Charles Dickens's
GREAT
EXPECTATIONS

Leonard Jenkin

1997 Barnes & Noble Books

MACMILLAN is a registered trademark of Macmillan, Inc.
Monarch and colophons are trademarks of Simon & Schuster, Inc.,
registered in the U.S. Patent and Trademark Office.

Macmillan Publishing USA
A division of Simon & Schuster, Inc.
1633 Broadway
New York, NY   10019

ISBN 0-7607-0820-7

Text design by Tony Meisel

Printed and bound in the United States of America.

00 01 M 9

RRDC

CONTENTS

INTRODUCTION TO CHARLES DICKENS

EARLY LIFE

Charles Dickens was born on February 7, 1812, in Portsea, England. His father, John Dickens, was a minor clerk in the Navy Pay Office; his father's parents had been servants and his mother's parents only slightly higher on the social scale. John Dickens was a happy-go-lucky, improvident man whose family was often in need as the debts piled up. At the age of twelve, Charles Dickens experienced what was to become the key event of his life. His father was imprisoned for debt in the Marshalsea Prison; young Charles was taken out of school and put to work in a blacking warehouse in London, pasting labels on bottles of shoe polish. Although he later returned to school for a time, this experience left a permanent mark on the soul of Charles Dickens. Even many years later, after he had become a successful author, he could not bear to talk about it, or be reminded of his family's shame.

At the age of fifteen, Dickens began working as an office boy for a law firm. He taught himself shorthand, and by 1828 he was a reporter for the lay courts of Doctors' Common. The dull routine of the legal profession never interested him, so he became a newspaper reporter for the *Mirror of Parliament*, *The True Sun*, and finally for the *Morning Chronicle*. (John Forster, later his closest friend and biographer, was also employed at *The True Sun*.) By the age of twenty, Dickens was one of the best Parliamentary reporters in all England.

During this same period Dickens' interest began to switch from journalism to literature. His first work of fiction, "Dinner at Poplar Walk" (later reprinted as "Mr. Minns and His Cousin"), appeared in the *Monthly Magazine* when he was twenty-one. His newspaper work had given him an intimate knowledge of the streets and byways of London, and late in 1832 he began writing sketches and stories of London life. These stories began to appear in periodicals and newspapers in 1833, and in 1836, they were gathered together as *Sketches by Boz, Illustrations of Every-day Life*, and *Every-day People*. This pseudonym, Boz, was suggested by his brother's pronunciation of "Moses" when he had a cold.

PICKWICK PAPERS

The success of the *Sketches* brought an invitation from the publishers Chapman and Hall in 1836 to furnish the "letter-press" for a series of cartoon sketches about a humorous cockney sporting club. (The letter-press was little more than a running accompaniment, like an ornamental border around the drawings.) The project had hardly begun when Robert Seymour, the artist, committed suicide. Dickens searched long for a new artist and found an ideal collaborator in H. K. Browne ("Phiz"). By this time Dickens had persuaded the publisher to let him improvise a fictional narrative, and, when the *Posthumous Papers of the Pickwick Club* finally came out, the story predominated over the illustrations.

When *Pickwick Papers* appeared in April 1836, as a monthly serial, the sales were at first discouraging. Of the first issue, a modest 400 copies were printed; later the work became increasingly popular. Some 40,000 copies of each issue were sold. After the last installment appeared in November 1837, the novel was published in book form. This set the pattern for all of Dickens' subsequent novels.

The success of *Pickwick* convinced Dickens that his real career lay in writing fiction; he gave up his Parliamentary reporting to devote himself full time to it. In 1836 he had married Catherine Hogarth, the daughter of one of the owners of the *Morning Chronicle*; his growing family made it necessary to work tirelessly at his writing. His next work, *Oliver Twist*, began appearing even before *Pickwick* was completed. *Nicholas Nickleby* followed in a like manner in 1838–1839, and the very first number sold some 50,000 copies. During this same period he was editor of *Bentley's Miscellany* (1837–

1839). By the 1840s Dickens had become the most popular novelist in Britain, taking over the place long held by Sir Walter Scott.

THE MIDDLE YEARS

The years between 1840 and 1855 were most fruitful ones: *The Old Curiosity Shop, Barnaby Rudge, A Christmas Carol, Martin Chuzzlewit, Dombey and Son, David Copperfield, Bleak House, Little Dorrit,* and *Hard Times* all appeared. In addition, Dickens made his first trip to America; copyright laws at that time allowed American publishers to pirate his works, and their lack of concern over this injustice undoubtedly contributed to Dickens' unfavorable criticism of America in *Martin Chuzzlewit.* In 1850 Dickens founded his own periodical, *Household Words,* and continued to edit it until he and his partner exchanged it for *All the Year Round* in 1859. *Hard Times, A Tale of Two Cities,* and *Great Expectations* appeared in serial form in these publications. But these years of literary success were marred by domestic strife. He and his wife had never been particularly suited to each other, and their marriage ended in separation in 1856.

In addition to writing, Dickens had another love—amateur theatricals—which led him into yet another pursuit in the latter part of his career. He gave public readings from his novels from 1859 to 1868 in England, Scotland, and America. He had always loved the theater—he studied drama as a young man and had organized an amateur theatrical company of his own in 1847 (he was both manager and principal actor).

His energies never seemed to fail: he burned the candle at both ends. He published *Our Mutual Friend* in 1864–1865, and at his death left an unfinished novel, *The Mystery of Edwin Drood,* a suspense tale in the nature of a detective story. He died suddenly in 1870 from a stroke at the age of fifty-eight. G. K. Chesterton once said that Dickens died of "popularity." It would seem so; his exhaustive burden (marked by insomnia and fatigue) is well catalogued in his letters. He was buried in the Poets' Corner of Westminster Abbey.

Dickens wrote with an eye on the tastes of a wide readership, never far ahead of the printer, and was always ready to modify the story to suit his readers. For example, when the sales of serial installments of *Martin Chuzzlewit* fell from 60,000 to 20,000, Dickens sent his hero off to America in order to stimulate renewed interest. No novelist ever had so close a relationship with his or her public, a public ranging from barely literate factory girls to wealthy dowagers, but consisting mostly of the newly formed middle classes.

TEACHER AND ENTERTAINER

Walter Allen in *The English Novel* points out that Dickens became the spokesperson for this rising middle class, and also its teacher. "Dickens more than any of his contemporaries was the expression of the conscience—untutored, baffled, muddled as it doubtless often was—of his age," he writes. Not only in his novels, but in his magazine, *Household Words*, Dickens lashed out at what he considered the worst social abuses of his time: imprisonment for debt, the ferocious penal code, the unsanitary slums that bred criminals, child labor, the widespread mistreatment of children, the unsafe machinery in factories, and the hideous schools.

Yet, as Allen suggests, Dickens was primarily a great entertainer, "the greatest entertainer, probably, in the history of fiction." It is significant that Dickens was not satisfied to have his books the best sellers of their time. He wanted to see his audience, to manipulate it with the power of his own words. His public readings gave him an excellent opportunity to do so. Sitting alone on a bare stage, he would read excerpts from various novels, act them out, imitating the voices of the various characters. These theatrical readings would always contain a dying-child scene or two, which left his audience limp and tear-stained. Dickens suffered all the emotions with his audience, even after repeated readings, and this undoubt-edly helped to shorten his life. He entertained his readers with humor, pathos, suspense, and melodrama, all on a grand scale. Charles Dickens had a fertile imagination that peopled his novels with characters and events that continue to enter-tain twentieth-century readers just as they delighted his contemporaries.

NOVEL TECHNIQUE

An understanding of Dickens as an artist requires an under-standing of the method of publication he used—monthly or weekly installments. Serialization left its mark on his fiction and often accounts for the flaws that many critics have found in his work. John Butt and Kathleen Tillotson in *Dickens at Work* (1957) describe the problems serial publication imposed:

Chapters must be balanced within a number in respect both of length and of effect. Each number must lead, if not to a climax, at least to a point of rest; and the rest between num-bers is necessarily more extended than what the mere chapter divisions provide. The writer had also to bear in mind that his readers were constantly interrupted for prolonged periods, and that he must take this into account in his characteriza-tions and, to some extent, in his plotting.

This technique brought on a loose, episodic treatment with a vast, intricate plot, numerous characters and much repetition to jog the reader's memory. Instead of the whole novel slowly building to a real climax, each part had to have a little climax of its own. In *Hard Times* the bad effects of serialization are at a minimum because it is a comparatively short novel (about 260 pages in most editions), and it appeared in weekly rather than monthly parts. But the careful reader can still tell where each part ended; considerations of space rather than of artis-tic technique formed the story.

The works of Dickens have many of their roots in the

eighteenth century, especially in the novels of Tobias Smollett, whom he greatly admired. From Smollett he borrowed many devices of characterization—"tagging" characters with physical peculiarities, speech mannerisms, compulsive gestures, and eccentric names. Examples in *Hard Times* include the distinctive speech pattern of Stephen Blackpool, who talks in a phonetically transcribed Lancashire dialect; the self-deprecating speech of Bounderby or the self-pitying talk of Mrs. Sparsit; the physical peculiarities of Bitzer, the epitome of pallidness; the names of characters—Bounderby, M'Choakumchild, Gradgrind—so evocative of their personalities.

The eighteenth century also brought the picaresque tradition in fiction to full flower. (The term refers to novels that depict the life of a picaro [Spanish: "rogue"] and that consist of unconnected episodes held together by the presence of the central character.) Early novels, especially those of Defoe, Fielding, and Smollett, were rambling, episodic, and anecdotal. Many of the novels of Dickens—*Pickwick, Oliver Twist, David Copperfield* to name a few—are picaresque in technique. *Hard Times* borrows from the tradition only the irreverent, satirical view of stuffed-shirt pretentiousness and of established society in general. The eighteenth-century theater, with its sharply defined villains, its involved melodramatic plots, and its farcical humor, also suggested ideas for plots and characterizations to Dickens.

Dickens took his descriptive techniques from Sir Walter Scott and other early nineteenth-century novelists. No character, no matter how minor, appears on the scene without being fully described, not only as to physical appearance, but as to the clothing he wears. Dickens also excels in the short but evocative description of places; in *Hard Times* the portrayal of the murky streets and factories of Coketown and of its blighted wasteland-like countryside are particularly notable.

THE WORLD OF HIS NOVELS

The world of Dickens' novels is a fantasy world, a fairy-tale world, a nightmare world. It is a world seen as through the eyes of a child: the shadows are blacker, the fog denser, the houses higher, the midnight streets emptier and more terrifying than in reality. To a child, inanimate objects have lives of their own: thus the smoke malevolently winds over Coketown like serpents, and the pistons of the steam engines in the factory are "melancholy mad elephants."

The characters, too, are seen as children see people. Their peculiarities are heightened to eccentricities; their vices, to monstrous proportions. Most of the people in his novels are caricatures, characterized by their externals, almost totally predictable in behavior. We know little about them beyond their surface behavior; Dickens focuses on the outward person, not the inner motives. It is interesting to note, however, that Dickens was able to create intensely individual portraits even though he lacked the ability to analyze motivation and character developments. His characters are more than types or mere abstract representations of virtue or vice. They are intensely alive and thus memorable. The characters from a Dickens novel are remembered long after the plots and even the titles of the books have been forgotten.

DICKENS THE REFORMER

Dickens in his lifetime saw Great Britain change from a rural, agricultural "Merrie Old England" of inns, stagecoaches, and fox-hunting squires to an urbanized, commercial-industrial land of railroads, factories, slums, and a city proletariat. These changes are chronicled in his novels, and it is possible to read them as a social history of England. *Pickwick*, although set in 1827–1828, reflects much of what still survived of the old eighteenth-century way of life. *Oliver Twist* (1837–1839) shows the first impact of the Industrial Revolution—the poverty existing at that time and the feeble attempt to remedy it by workhouses. *Dombey and Son* (1846–1848) describes the coming of the railroad, a symbol of change. Dombey, the merchant, sacrifices love, wife, and children for a position of power through money; yet he is already obsolete, for the industrialist is the ruler now.

Dickens grew increasingly bitter with each novel; his criticism of society became more radical, his satire more biting and less sweetened by humor. In his later novels he often broke out in indignant exasperation and almost hysterical anger. He figuratively mounted a soapbox, demanding that the "Lords and Gentlemen" do something about the appalling conditions of the poor.

In his early novels, society itself is not evil; it is only some people who are bad and who create misery for others by their callousness and neglect. By the time of *Dombey and Son*, it is institutions that are evil, representing in that novel the self-expanding power of accumulated money. *Bleak House* (1852–1853) attacks the law's delay and the self-perpetuating mass of futility it has become. *Hard Times* (1854) savagely lampoons the economic theories that Dickens considered responsible for much of human misery. The English historian, Lord Macaulay, charged that it was full of "sullen Socialism." Of *Little Dorrit* (1855–1857), which attacks prisons and imprisonment for debt, George Bernard Shaw said that it was "more seditious than Karl Marx." In *Our Mutual Friend* (1864–1865) we see the fully disillusioned Dickens. The atmosphere of the novel is grim, permeated with a sense of growing nightmare. There is the feeling that something deep and basic is wrong with the social order, something beyond the mere reforming of bad people or poorly run institutions.

T. A. Jackson in *Charles Dickens: The Progress of a Radical* tries to claim him for the Marxists as a champion of the downtrodden masses. Yet Lenin, the father of Communist Russia, found Dickens intolerable in his "middle-class sentimentality." George Orwell was probably correct when he stated that

Dickens' criticism of society was neither political nor economic, but moral. Certainly Dickens offered no substitutes for the system or institutions he attacked. Thus, in *A Tale of Two Cities* (1859) he expressed his loathing for the decadent French aristocracy of the ancient regime, but he seemed to like the triumphant democracy of the Revolution no better. In *Hard Times* he criticizes the exploitation of the industrial workers by the factory owners, but he is repelled almost equally by the attempt of the workers to form unions in self-defense. He seems to suggest that the Golden Rule is the only solution to class struggle.

GREAT EXPECTATIONS
BRIEF SUMMARY

INTRODUCTION

STAGE ONE

Alone by his parents' tombstones in the churchyard, young Pip (Philip Pirrip) is frightened by the appearance, out of the desolate marsh country, of a convict in shackles who makes Pip promise to bring him food and a file the next morning. Pip does so, robbing the pantry of Mrs. Joe Gargery, his shrewish sister who has brought him up near the forge of her husband, a blacksmith. The convict eagerly devours his food, and Pip leaves him (after telling him that he met another convict on the marsh that morning). Later that day, soldiers arrive at the Gargery house, and Pip and Joe (his brother-in-law) go with them and see the convicts both retaken as they are struggling with one another in a ditch. Some time afterward, Pip receives an invitation, from his pompous Uncle Pumblechook, to go to eccentric old Miss Havisham's house. Once there, Pip notes the darkness and oldness of everything surrounding Miss Havisham and meets the proud Estella (a girl his own age) who makes him feel coarse and common. Soon after, Pip goes again to Miss Havisham's and sees some of her relations. He also has a fight with a pale young man; victory in this earns him a kiss from Estella. After this visit, Pip is soon apprenticed to Joe, but, having met Estella and Miss Havisham, he does not care for work at the forge as much as he had thought he would. Joe Gargery and Orlick, a helper at the forge, have a fight, and that evening, Mrs. Joe receives a serious injury from unknown hands. Pip's desire to become a gentleman grows in him, and he tells Joe's housekeeper, Biddy, about it. One evening, a Mr. Jaggers comes to Joe and Pip and explains that Pip has great expectations and that he is being given money by a person wishing to remain unknown so that he may become a gentleman. Pip soon orders new clothes, takes sorrowful leave of Joe and Biddy, says good-bye to Miss

Havisham (whom he thinks of as his benefactress), and starts for London.

STAGE TWO

In London, Pip sees Mr. Jaggers, who is a lawyer, and his clerk, Wemmick, who takes him to stay with the son of his tutor-to-be. Pip recognizes his roommate, Herbert Pocket, as the pale young man with whom he once fought. He soon meets his tutor, Matthew Pocket, and Pocket's family, with whom he goes to live. He accepts an invitation from Wemmick and visits him at his home, seeing the non-business side of Jaggers' clerk. Jaggers also invites him to dinner, along with his fellow students at Mr. Pocket's. One of these students, a surly fellow named Bentley Drummle, quarrels with Pip. Joe comes to see Pip in London and Pip, feeling superior, is unable to make him feel at home. Soon after, Pip visits Estella, whom he loves, at Miss Havisham's. He is more attracted to her than ever. He is also, along with Herbert Pocket, falling into debt. At this point, his sister, Mrs. Joe, dies, and Pip attends the funeral where he talks seriously with Biddy. Once back in London, Pip secretly sets his friend Herbert up in business. Estella comes to London where Pip sees her frequently, although she seems to encourage the attentions of Bentley Drummle. At this place in the tale, Pip is visited by the convict whom he helped on the marsh long ago and learns the true source of the money that has helped him with his expectations. The convict's name is Magwitch, and it is he who has been responsible for Pip's becoming a gentleman. Pip also learns that if Magwitch is caught in England, it means his death.

STAGE THREE

Magwitch, who calls himself Provis, is proud of and affection-ate toward the gentleman he has made. In his telling of his life, we learn that the other convict Compeyson (who is Magwitch's bitter enemy), is the man whose treachery has led Miss Havisham to her present mode of life. Pip then visits

Miss Havisham where he learns that Estella will soon be married to Bentley Drummle. Upon returning to London, Pip learns (from Wemmick) that Compeyson is watching Magwitch. He and Herbert take Magwitch to the house in which Herbert's wife-to-be, Clara Barley, lives. At this time, Pip discovers that Molly (Jaggers' housekeeper) is Estella's mother and that Magwitch is her father. Soon, he receives word from Wemmick that the time has come to try to smuggle Magwitch out of England, using a plan they had previously made. Pip also receives a mysterious note saying that he is to go to the old lime-kiln on the marshes if he wishes to learn something concerning Provis. He goes and is attacked by Orlick, now in league with Compeyson. It is Orlick who had previously injured Mrs. Joe. Pip would have been killed if not for the intervention of Herbert and some other friends. Pip and Herbert row Magwitch out on the river the next day in order to catch an outward bound ship. Compeyson and policemen, in another boat, order them to stop. Magwitch grabs Compeyson, and as they are run down by a steamer, Compeyson is drowned. Magwitch is severely injured and taken by the police. Herbert soon leaves London on business, and Pip tenderly nurses Magwitch, who dies before his death penalty can be carried out. After these events, Pip falls into deliriousness and is nursed by faithful Joe, from whom he learns that Miss Havisham is dead. Joe leaves as Pip becomes well again. Pip resolves to go home, make amends to Joe, and offer himself to Biddy. He arrives only to find them celebrating their wedding day. Pip joins Herbert abroad, and, after eleven years, he returns and visits the ruins of Miss Havisham's house. Here he again meets Estella, who is now a widow. They both have grown older and wiser through much suffering, and as they walk away together, Pip sees "no shadow of another parting from her."

CAST OF CHARACTERS

A novel by Dickens usually contains many characters and *Great Expectations* is no exception. The list of characters given here presents only the most basic information about each. The major figures in the novel are dealt with in detail in the Character Analyses section.

MARSH COUNTRY GROUP

Pip. The narrator and hero of the story. Herbert Pocket's judgment is a fair one. "A good fellow, with impetuosity and hesitation, boldness and diffidence, action and dreaming, curiously mixed in him."

Joe Gargery. A "gentle Christian man." He is Pip's boyhood companion and is faithful to him in his greatest need. He is Dickens' symbol of everything good from which Pip turns away.

Mrs. Joe Gargery. Pip's sister, more than twenty years his senior. She is a thorough shrew, whom Orlick chooses as a victim in his revenge.

Mr. Pumblechook. A well-to-do corn and seed merchant. He is Joe's uncle. He is pompous, bullying, hypocritical, self-righteous, and sycophantic, depending upon circumstances

Mr. Wopsle. A townsman of Pip's. He aspires to the stage and so goes to London. He is never modest about his abilities.

Mr. Wopsle's Great Aunt. A senile schoolteacher.

Biddy. At first, Joe's housekeeper, then, his wife. She understands Pip very well and their conversations reveal his motives and feelings.

Mr. and Mrs. Hubble. Friends of the Gargerys.

Mr. Trabb. The town tailor.

Trabb's Boy. Trabb's young helper who mocks Pip and, later in life, helps to rescue him from danger.

Orlick. A worker employed at the forge by Joe. He attacks Mrs. Joe to gain vengeance and, eventually, allies himself with Compeyson and threatens Pip's life.

SATIS HOUSE GROUP

Miss Havisham. Pip's supposed benefactress. Deserted on her wedding day, she lives in a world where time has stopped. She raises Estella to gain vengeance for the wrong done her.

Estella. Miss Havisham's adopted child. She is, at first, a creature of vengeance but, finally, reconciles herself with Pip as the tale ends. This lovely, cold woman is the moving force behind the tale's central action.

Miss Georgiana Pocket, Miss Sarah Pocket, Mrs. Camilla, Mr. Raymond. All relatives of Miss Havisham. They are humbugs who claim to care for her but only seek her money.

LONDON GROUP

Herbert Pocket. The son of Matthew Pocket and Pip's close friend.

Mr. Matthew Pocket. Herbert's father and Pip's tutor. He is a gentleman who is quite confused by his family; he is honest and kindly.

Mrs. Pocket. Herbert's mother, wife to Matthew. She is a woman who ignores her family to dream of her supposedly noble lineage.

Flopson, Millers. Nurses in the Pocket household.

Mrs. Coiler. An overly sympathetic neighbor of the Pockets.

Mr. Jaggers. A criminal lawyer and Pip's guardian. He is a burly, forceful and stern man, without business scruples or peer in his field.

Molly. Mr. Jaggers' housekeeper and Estella's mother. She is a pale, nervous, fierce-looking woman.

John Wemmick. Mr. Jaggers' right-hand man. Wemmick's life is carefully divided between his home and his business, and he is a different person in each place. In his private capacity, he helps Pip with his problems.

Aged Parent. Wemmick's deaf but lively father. He figures in some of the story's most delightful sequences.

Miss Skiffins. Wemmick's lady friend; later, his wife.

Bentley Drummle. A sulky, unfriendly fellow student of Pip's. He marries Estella and treats her cruelly.

Startop. A bright young man with a delicate face. He is a fellow student with Pip in the Pocket household.

Mrs. Brandley. A widow lady at Richmond with whom Estella is placed in order to take advantage of her social connections.

Clara Barley. Herbert Pocket's pretty fiancée, whom he later marries.

Mr. Barley. Clara's father. He is a bedridden, noisy, drunken ex-purser.

Mrs. Whimple. The Barley's landlady. She is an elderly woman and an excellent housewife.

The Avenger. Young servant to Pip and Herbert.

Clarriker. A young merchant whom Pip meets through Miss Skiffins.

CONVICTS
Abel Magwitch. The true source of the money for Pip's expectations. He is a fierce, crude man who wishes to make Pip a gentleman for his own reasons as well as in gratitude. His character changes while he is in England for the last time, and Pip nurses him until his death.

Compeyson. The novel's darkest villain. He is the man who was Miss Havisham's false lover and also, the betrayer of Magwitch when they were partners. In his final attempt to eliminate Magwitch, he is drowned in their struggle as a steamer runs over their boats.

DETAILED ANALYSIS: STAGE ONE

CHAPTER 1

The central character and narrator of *Great Expectations* was born with the name of Philip Pirrip. As he tells us, he could not, as a child, pronounce his name, so he called himself, and came to be called, Pip. He has no memory of his parents and can only guess what they were like by the appearance of their carved tombstones in the churchyard near the marshes not far from his village. Pip's first memory is of contemplating these tombstones on a cold, damp day; only to be interrupted by a mud-soaked, shackled, fearful man in gray who leaps from behind a tombstone, grabs him, and demands to know his name. Pip gives his name in terror, is turned upside down to empty his pockets, and is then set on top of a tombstone. Hungrily, the man eats the bread he has found in Pip's pockets, and after threatening to eat the boy himself, he proceeds to question him. Pip explains that he lives with his sister and her husband, Joe Gargery, the blacksmith. At this the man takes hold of him again and threatens to cut out and eat his heart and liver if Pip does not do as he asks. Early the next morning, the boy is told to come to the old gun battery in the marsh and to bring a file and "wittles" (victuals, or food). He is instructed to tell no one about their meeting. For this frightening man has a friend, a younger man, who will find Pip even if he is warm in his bed, and will creep in and tear him open. For fear of this, Pip promises. He is then released and begins to go home; but, fascinated despite his fear, he turns to watch the man as he limps away. As he crosses the graveyard, his cautious gait seems to Pip like that of a man avoiding the hands of the dead, which reach up invisibly to pull victims into their graves. The marshes stretch flat and dark toward the river and the remnants of a red sunset. The sky is pierced only by a beacon for sailors and a gallows on which a pirate was hung by chains. As the man crosses the marsh slowly, he seems like that pirate come alive. At this thought, Pip takes fright again and runs home.

COMMENT

Dickens wrote only two novels narrated in the first person, and one of these is *Great Expectations*. By this device, the reader is immediately and intimately involved with the main character and his actions. This character is Pip; not only are we vividly involved in what happens to him but also in how he thinks, reacts, and sees. The following will prove important throughout Pip's narrative. First, Pip is an orphan which means that he has no social position, nor any expectations for his own future. In a sense, to be an orphan is to be estranged from the normal structure of society. Secondly, he is impressionable and imaginative. The stranger easily inspires fear in the young boy; to the extent that Pip sees him, first, as pursued by the hands of the dead and, then, as the dreadful ghost of a pirate. The appearance of the grim man with the iron on his leg does have all the threatening qualities of a ghost. The eerie, visionary aspects of the scene are enhanced by the flat marsh and the fog. The beacon and the gallows appear in this landscape like symbols of wandering, crime, and death.

CHAPTER 2

Pip's sister, Mrs. Joe Gargery, is more than twenty years his senior; a tall bony, black-haired woman with skin so coarsely red that it seems to Pip that she must wash it with a grater rather than with soap. The work apron which she seems never to remove is worn with an air of reproachful martyrdom. Mrs. Joe has earned the respect of the neighbors by bringing up the orphaned Pip "by hand" and, to the boy, this means that the hand is laid on him hard, heavy, and often . . . and on her husband as well for Joe Gargery is a "Hercules in strength, but also in weakness." He is a sweet-natured, easy-going man with blond hair and eyes of an indeterminate blue. His forge adjoins their wooden house and, when Pip arrives home, he finds Joe alone in the kitchen. Mrs. Joe has gone out a dozen times looking for Pip and, this time, she left taking "Tickler."

This is the cane with which she "tickles" Pip's behind in moments of anger. As Joe puts it, she is on "the Ram-page," and, sure enough, she enters and tickles Pip well before even asking where he has been. When she hears where, she declares that, between Pip and Joe, she is being driven to her grave in that churchyard; she then sets about angrily preparing tea. Pip dares not eat his bread and butter for fear that he may not be able to get anything else for the man at the marshes. With Joe as his companion and fellow sufferer, this is difficult for it is their custom to compare the progress of their bites into the slices. Joe is worried that Pip isn't eating his but when, after a few minutes of inattention, he turns to find Pip's bread gone, he is astounded and even more concerned less the boy choke. He declares that he has never seen Pip's equal at bolting food. Hearing this, Mrs. Joe grabs both husband and boy and gives each a dose of unpleasant Tar-water. The medicine is punishment enough but Pip is suffering doubly now. The bread and butter that disappeared so rapidly down the leg of his trousers is slipping, and he must grasp it firmly each time he moves. In addition, his conscience plagues him for robbing Mrs. Joe, and his imagination tells him that, perhaps, the man is just outside and wants his bread now. As tomorrow is Christmas, it is Pip's task to stir the pudding for an hour; this proves difficult while clutching the bread in his trouser leg. Happily, the chance to slip away comes, and he deposits the bread in his bedroom. As he finishes stirring the pudding, the great guns on the Battery in the marshes are heard. Pip asks why and is told that the firing serves as a warning that another convict has escaped from the Hulks. Joe tries silently to mouth an explanation of the words "convicts" and "Hulks," but Pip cannot understand. He exasperates Mrs. Joe by asking aloud, and he learns that the Hulks are the prison ships moored at the marshes and convicts are robbers and murderers who started out by asking questions and ended up by getting caught. Feeling that he is surely going to be a convict (as he has already robbed Mrs. Joe and asked questions), Pip goes off to bed. He is in mortal terror at his promise, the man to whom he made it, and his punishing sister. He dreams he is floating down the river toward the Hulks, and the ghostly pirate is calling to him to come and be hanged now instead of putting it off. He wakes at dawn; full of the fearful knowledge that he must rob the pantry. He takes cheese, meat, a pork pie, and some brandy restoring the bottle to its former level by diluting it with the contents of a jug from the kitchen. Taking a file from the forge, Pip sets off at a run for the marshes.

COMMENT

Pip seems to sense that the strange man he has met on the marshes is an escaped convict. His waking and sleeping mind is tormented with fear and with the pangs of conscience for deceiving Joe and Mrs. Joe. Guilt and fear have begun to intrude on his innocence.

We see Joe and Mrs. Joe with the vividness of a young boy's perception. Mrs. Joe is a harsh woman who persecutes her family physically, in fits of temper, and mentally, by assuming an air of martyrdom that accuses both Pip and Joe of making her miserable. It is from Joe that Pip receives his share of love. The gentle blacksmith does his best to warn the boy of impending onslaughts from the cane. The extent to which they are comrades is shown in their sharing the ritual of eating bread bite by bite.

CHAPTER 3

The morning seems as damp to Pip as the handkerchief of a goblin who has cried all night. The mist makes it even more threatening, obscuring the dykes on the marsh so that they loom up before him at the last moment. Pip believes that each form accuses him of theft. The cold makes him feel that his feet are bound in iron like those of the man he is looking for. Finding him suddenly, asleep in the fog, Pip touches the stranger to wake him. The gray suit, the iron-bound leg, everything about this seems right but the face is not the same.

This new convict swears, tries to hit Pip, and then runs off into the mist. He must be the young man who would eat Pip's heart and liver. Pip finds the right convict soon; he is waiting for him at the Battery and is shivering with the cold of a night on the marshes. Sympathetically, Pip gives him the file, the food and the brandy; saying that he hopes the man hasn't caught a chill. The man bolts down the food like a hungry dog, scarcely stopping to chew and looks around suspiciously all the while. Pip assures him that he hasn't brought anyone with him but suggests that, perhaps, the young man would want some food, too. The convict laughs this off until he hears the boy's description of meeting another man (identically dressed but with a scarred cheek) also on the marsh. The convict's night on the wet flats has been so full of soldiers, guns, and pursuing feet that he believed the cannon fire indicating another escaped convict to be part of these delusions. Pip points out the direction the second man took. At this, the convict becomes full of fierce hurry. He stuffs the remaining food in his shirt and, in a frenzy, sets to work with the file. This return of viciousness frightens Pip. He remembers that he should return home before they miss him. The convict is now engrossed in filing; he ignores Pip. The boy goes off, and the last thing he hears through the mist is the sound of the file against iron.

COMMENT

Guilt has been awakened in Pip's conscience. His reactions to the mist are full of it; still, the boy shows real sympathy for the convict who is suffering from cold and hunger. The convict himself, although he is wary, seems to trust Pip and feel grateful toward him. For a short time, there is a bond between them, and it is only broken by the man's evident frenzy at the news that there is another convict loose nearby. Pip's guilty theft of food and his dreams of being a convict account somewhat for the easier feeling between the two. The quality of dream is again enhanced by the mist and by the brief appearance of still a third guilty person. As Pip loses innocence, these brief meetings on the marsh will seem like a nightmare. We may expect this, for Dickens enhances the confusion and mystery of the scene by vague images of phantoms and goblins; by the threat of pursuit and the convict's guilty fear and by the ever-present marsh fog. Fog becomes an image for Pip's confusion and fear. Convicts and prison become a theme.

CHAPTER 4

When Pip arrives home, Mrs. Joe is cleaning the house furiously in preparation for Christmas guests. The stolen food has not been missed. His conscience weighing heavily, Pip explains his absence by saying that he went to hear the Christmas carols; this proves acceptable. Mrs. Joe comments only that she might have gone too, if she weren't "a slave with her apron never off." She returns to her cleaning; even taking the protective coverings from the rarely used parlor. By crossing his fingers, Joe indicates to Pip that she is in a cross temper, and Pip observes to himself that his sister has a way of making cleanliness more uncomfortable than dirt. Pip and Joe are to go to church. Joe looks like a scarecrow in penitential dress, and Pip wears a suit that restricts the movement of his limbs as much as Mrs. Joe could wish. His inner remorse and terror, however, are his greatest punishment and Pip speculates as to whether or not the church could protect him from the terrible young man if he were to confess his deed. When he and Joe return from church, everything is ready for the guests, and the theft is still undiscovered. The expected guests arrive. Mr. Wopsle, the clerk of the church, who is a man with an uncommonly deep voice of which he is uncommonly proud, comes first. Mr. Hubble, a sawdusty gentleman who is the village wheelmaker, arrives next, with his curly-headed wife. Uncle Pumblechook, a relatively well-to-do man whom Pip is not permitted to call uncle, comes, bringing, as he does each Christmas, two bottles of wine. He is thanked effusively, as always, by Mrs. Joe. After a theatrical grace by Mr. Wopsle, the company sits down to dinner. Pip is seated at the corner, squeezed in with Mr. Pumblechook's elbow in his eye, and given the worst scraps of the food. This he could bear, were he then ignored, but he is not. On this occasion, the grace is no sooner finished than he is told by all to be grateful, and the company decides that the lack of this virtue in the young is due to natural viciousness. To comfort Pip, as is his custom, Joe spoons a large portion of gravy onto the boy's plate. Mr. Wopsle now launches into a discussion of the grand sermon he would have given if the church were "thrown open," meaning, to competition. He concludes by giving a short sample sermon, condemning greed and gluttony and glaring at Pip as he observes that what is detestable in a pig is worse in a boy. Joe is ready with the gravy while Pumblechook takes the opportunity to impress upon the boy again what evil fate and early death would have visited him if his relatives had not chosen to bring him up by hand. In celebration of this, Mrs. Joe offers Pumblechook some brandy. This causes, in Pip, a spasm of fear that they will notice it is watered. The reaction is far worse for Uncle Pumblechook leaps up with bursts of coughing and runs for the door. Pip had refilled the brandy from the Tar-water bottles; however, in the rush to make Uncle comfortable, accusations are forgotten. Pip has just relaxed from his terror when he has occasion to panic again. With ceremony, Mrs. Joe goes to fetch Uncle Pumblechook's third gift; a pork pie. The horror of his theft overwhelms Pip. He does not know whether he actually shrieks or simply feels like shrieking, but he jumps from his seat and runs terrified to the door. There, he runs into a party of soldiers entering. They carry guns and one, holding handcuffs, seemingly about to take Pip into custody.

COMMENT

Again, Pip's guilt pervades all he sees. The warmth of his companionship with Joe is stressed by Joe's constant serving of gravy. At the same time, we are reminded by the company's conversation that Pip is an outsider;

isolated from the world by being an orphan which, in itself, seems to be a transgression of moral law. He is indebted to the world for whatever it may give him; even his Sunday suit is a means of punishing him. This enforced role cannot help but affect Pip's later actions. Guilt and gratitude are keynotes of his development. The plagues of his conscience, both the dream and his imaginings, come to an abrupt climax when, fearing discovery, he flees to the door only to find that soldiers have come to arrest him. In his state, he does not doubt that his theft may have been discovered by powers of law and order greater even than his sister. For us, the soldiers reinforce the hallucinatory aspects of Pip's previous adventures on the marsh. They continue the themes of crime and punishment, penance, and prison that have already been introduced.

CHAPTER 5

The "apparition" of soldiers attracts everyone and the ensuing confusion causes Mrs. Joe to forget about her missing pie. Pip recovers from his shock and learns that the soldiers have come in search of the blacksmith. The handcuffs are in need of repair, and Joe immediately sets to work, lighting the forge. The soldiers have instructions to encircle and arrest at dusk a pair of escaped convicts on the marshes. They will need the handcuffs then. Mr. Pumblechook offers his wine around. The sergeant's flattering hints that such a fine beverage could only have been provided by a man such as Pumblechook wake that man's generosity and joviality. The entire company gathers around the roaring fire and merrily consumes both bottles of wine as they discuss the forthcoming arrest. It seems to Pip that the flames and the shadows they make on the walls shake in menace at the convict he pities and that even the light of the afternoon has paled sympathetically at the threat. When Joe is finished, he suggests that he and Pip go along on the hunt; an idea that Mrs. Joe agrees to only because she is curious. As they follow behind the soldiers, Pip whispers to Joe that he hopes they will fail to find the convicts. Joe answers that he hopes, also, that the men will escape. As they tramp on through the sleet and rain, Pip, riding on Joe's back, hopes desperately that his convict (upon seeing him with the soldiers) will not believe him guilty of betrayal. The group has just neared the Battery when the sound of shouting voices reaches them on the wind and they start at a run towards the sound. As the cries become clearer, the words "murder" and "runaway convicts" reach Pip's ears. They come upon the convicts who are fighting and swearing viciously at one another in the bottom of a ditch. Pip's convict (he has come to call the man "my convict") insists plainly that he has kept the other man from escaping and is turning him in to the authorities. Between gasps for breath, the other man accuses Pip's convict of murder. The soldiers do not care one way or another, but the two raving men gradually make their story clear. Pip's convict had got clear of the Hulks and the other, the gentleman convict "followed his example." When Pip's convict discovered the other (whom he hated) on the marsh, he was enraged at the man's efforts to profit yet another time at his expense. Feeling that prison was worse than death, he detained the "gentleman," and he denies the accusation of murder. The second convict is clearly frightened and cannot look Pip's convict in the eyes. As the men are bound up, Pip's convict sees the boy, and Pip makes a shy gesture to assure him that he was not betrayed. The convict's return glance is full of attention. There follows a long trek across the black marshes, red torches lighting the way, until they reach the dock at which the prison ship will land. Pip's convict never looks at him again, but, while warming himself at a fire in the guard's house near the dock, he speaks to the sergeant. He wishes to confess, he says, to having stolen some food from the blacksmith's house, and he says it now because the confession will have no meaning later. Being told that Joe is the blacksmith, he apologizes for what hunger drove him to. Joe replies that, though he doesn't know why the man is a convict, he certainly wouldn't want "a poor miserable fellow-creature" starved for it. At this, the convict turns away, and Pip hears the sound of sobs in the man's throat. The rowboat comes to take Pip's convict out to the iron-clad prison ship. As Pip watches him climb aboard, the torches are thrown into the water as if to say it is all over with the convict.

COMMENT

The theme of convicts, guilt, and penitentiary continues to be central to the narrative in this scene where the convicts are captured and returned to the Hulks. Pip's allegiance to the man comes back to him. He calls him "my convict." He is sad to think that he might be thought guilty of betrayal and does his best to assure his convict that he is innocent. Here, guilt and innocence refer to a reverse order of things; based on human sympathy with an outcast rather than on the written law that turns people into outcasts. Both Pip and Joe are innocent in their human feelings, and it is this fact and their sympathy that bring tears to the convict. The scene is again depicted as an "apparition," an illusion, that is more impressively real than the facades of such men as Pumblechook in the previous scene. This is enhanced by the fire in the dark forge and, again, by the torches on the marsh. Fire becomes a linking image in the book. The evident and fierce hatred of Pip's convict for the other, the "gentleman" who apparently wronged him, is also significant in the subsequent development of the plot. Being a gentleman is apparently not entirely desirable.

CHAPTER 6

It has been a long day and, as Pip is weary, Joe takes him on his back and carries him home. The guests are still there and, upon hearing Joe's account of the theft of food, they devote some energy to conjectures as to how the convict got into the house. Mr. Pumblechook's notion that, perhaps, he came down the kitchen chimney is accepted and Pip is hauled off to bed by Mrs. Joe. Now that the truth about the missing food is in no danger of being discovered by his sister, Pip's conscience ceases to bother him on her account. However, he does feel guilty about not telling Joe the whole truth; especially when he sees the blacksmith hunting for his file. Pip loves Joe because Joe allows him to, and the prospect of both of them suffering in the future from the shadow of suspicion is too much for the boy. Just as Pip was too cowardly to avoid the theft (although he knew it was wrong) he is now too cowardly to make clean breast of it, although he knows this would be right.

COMMENT

Fear of Joe's disapproval has started Pip on the path that will corrupt his innocence. In continuing the deception, the boy is erecting his first facade. He does not know that this facade will later cause a serious separation between himself and Joe.

CHAPTER 7

Pip's education progresses slowly. Soon after the incident on the marsh, he becomes Joe's apprentice in the forge and begins doing odd jobs for the neighbors. The small wages he earns are kept in a box on a high kitchen shelf, and Mrs. Joe makes sure that the boy never sees them. In doing so, she zealously believed that she was saving Pip from being "Pompeyed," that is, pampered. Every evening, between six and seven, Pip goes to school at the cottage of Mr. Wopsle's great-aunt, a little, aged person who usually falls asleep during the lesson. The aunt also keeps a disorganized general store in the same room. Pip soon discovers that it is Biddy, an unkempt little girl related in some way to the aunt and orphaned like himself, who runs the store and does most of the teaching. One evening, having vaguely mastered the alphabet with Biddy's help, Pip sits by a fire in Joe's cottage and manages, after an hour or two, to compose a note to Joe. He presents the smeared slate to Joe who is sitting beside him. Joe is delighted to find his own name written there but can read nothing else. He does not know how to read and derives all his pleasure along those lines from searching out the letters that spell his name. He explains that the neglect in his education arose from his father's partiality to alcohol, which led him to "hammer" Joe's mother and himself. As a result, Joe went to work as a blacksmith early in life, giving over his earnings to his parents. Joe, however, is emphatic about his father having been a good man at heart, and he recites the couplet he had made up when his father died: "Whatsume'er the failings on his part, Remember reader he were that good in his hart." The expense of taking care of his mother had prevented Joe from having this carved on the tombstone. Joe's mother had died not long after, however, and it was then that Joe met and married Mrs. Joe, whom he considers a "fine figure of a woman," adding that her redness and boniness do not signify anything. Pip was then but a baby and, when Joe proposed to the Missus, he made sure that the poor orphan would be coming along too. At this, Pip bursts out crying and hugs Joe who replies affectionately that the two of them are "ever the best of friends." Pip has offered in his note to teach Joe, and Joe now explains that any educating must proceed on the sly; Mrs. Joe would take such activities as a sign of rebellion in her husband for Mrs. Joe is given to "governing" both Joe and Pip and she would not appreciate Joe's efforts to rise. She is, as Joe puts it, a "master mind," by which he means that she must be the dominant one in the household. Joe remembers the trials and sufferings of his own mother at the hands of his father, and he would rather be inconvenienced himself than to subject Mrs. Joe to anything of the kind. He is sorry only that Pip has to bear the brunt of "Tickler." If he could, Joe would take all the beatings upon himself.

As Joe's speech (punctuated by gestures with the fire-poker) comes to an end, the two set about straightening up the house in preparation for Mrs. Joe's return. She has been to market with Uncle Pumblechook in his horse-drawn cart, and she is expected back soon. It is a dry, cold night, and Pip thinks how terrible it would be on the marshes tonight, dying of cold with the pitiless, useless stars looking on. The bells of Pumblechook's trotting mare are soon heard. Mrs. Joe and Pumblechook come in and warm themselves at the fire. She has big news for which, she announces, Pip must surely be grateful. She reveals that Miss Havisham wants Pip to come to her house to play. Miss Havisham, Pip remembers, is a very rich, grim, old lady who lives a life of seclusion in a large old house, firmly barricaded against robbers and situated at the end of town. Uncle Pumblechook is her tenant and, at her request that he find a boy to come and play, he has chosen Pip. This may be the making of Pip's fortune. Pip is to go with Pumblechook, stay the night at his house, and be taken to Miss Havisham the next morning. So saying, Mrs. Joe pounces on Pip, scrubs him vigorously all over with soap, towels him roughly, trusses him in stiff underclothes and his tightest suit, and then turns him over to Uncle, who stands by like a sheriff. After a short reminder to the boy to be grateful, Pip is set on the cart. He has barely had time to say good-bye to Joe (from whom he has never parted before), and he has no idea what will be expected of him tomorrow morning.

COMMENT

Education is the theme here. Its representatives in Pip's little world are Mr. Wopsle and his great-aunt; the former being ridiculously pompous, the latter simply unqualified. Yet, even at this early age, Pip is impressed by education as a mark of distinction. This attitude was probably impressed upon him by Mrs. Joe, who is far more conscious of such worldly measures of dignity than her husband. Dickens has made it clear, by contrasting the absurdity of Mr. Wopsle and his aunt with the simplicity of the totally uneducated blacksmith, that learning is no mark of dignity. Joe's speech is full of humility and warmth that show far greater human dignity than do the poses of Mr. Wopsle. He takes no offense at Pip's effort to help him "rise," but we do notice, at first, a hint of condescension in Pip. It is a quality we do not like, and it is quickly overwhelmed by Pip's loving tears at Joe's account of his life. The theme of rising fortune and worldly advancement finds expression again in the attitude of Mrs. Joe and Uncle Pumblechook to Pip's impending visit to Miss Havisham's. Clearly, something of the sort is being prepared for Pip. He does not yet see the advantages, however, for Miss Havisham's prison-like house and the tight clothing he must wear seem to Pip more like punishments than promises of future opportunities. The chapter ends with this recurrence of the theme of punishment and prison.

CHAPTER 8

Pip spends the night at Mr. Pumblechook's, where he sleeps in the attic. In the morning, he has some time to explore Pumblechook's seed store and is intrigued by the multitude of small drawers he finds there. Upon discovering that each contains packets of different seeds, he wonders whether the seeds ever long (on fine days) to break out of their little jails and bloom. Breakfast consists of little bread, less butter, watered milk, and arithmetic. The dismal aspect of doing addition between bites, while Pumblechook simply fires the questions and gorges on bacon, makes Pip aware that the Uncle's attitude toward him is much the same as Mrs. Joe's: that of an agent inflicting mortification and penitence. It is enough to make Pip happy when they start out for Miss Havisham's, although he has some misgivings about the visit. The old brick house, with its downstairs windows boarded up or barred with iron, is not a promising sight. There is also an unused brewery at the side. Their ring at the barred court-yard gate brings forth a very pretty, proud young lady. Pip is introduced and enters, but the girl makes it clear that Mr. Pumblechook's presence is not desired. His dignity ruffled, Pumblechook retreats. The wind seems colder within the court-yard. Pointing to the open, empty brewery, the girl remarks to

Pip that all the beer from that place would not hurt him but that, if any beer were made on the premises, it would probably be sour. Carelessly calling Pip "boy," the girl reveals that the name of the mansion is Satis House, which means Enough House, and was supposed to indicate that whoever owned it could want no more. Although she is Pip's age, the girl seems much older to Pip and treats him with scorn. The pair enter Satis House, and she lights his way with a candle through the dark hallways to a door, where she leaves him. Half-afraid, he knocks and enters. The room within is darkened against the daylight outside and lit with candles. It seems to be a dressing room, and the most prominent piece of furniture is a dressing table with a mirror. Sitting at it is a lady dressed richly (all in white) with a bridal veil, flowers, and jewels. Apparently, she has not finished dressing for her other shoe is on the table and, with it, more jewels and gloves. Her veil is not completely arranged, and the room is full of half-packed trunks. What surprises Pip is that everything that should have been white is actually yellow with age. The bride's hair is white, her eyes sunken, and her figure withered so that the dress no longer fits. Pip is reminded of a waxwork and a skeleton, but the form speaks and calls him over to be looked at. He is afraid to look at this lady, who is Miss Havisham, but notices that her watch has stopped at twenty minutes before nine. To her question as to whether he is afraid to look at a woman who has not seen the sun for so long, Pip lies and says that he is not. Miss Havisham tells him, with something near a weird boast, that her heart is broken. She wants some diversion and she commands Pip to play. He cannot, however, and explains he is not able to do so because of the strangeness and sadness of this new place. She then tells him to call Estella, the proud girl who greeted him at the gate. Pip does this with the sense that it is a "dreadful liberty" to shout her name so. When she comes, Miss Havisham commands them to play cards. To Estella's retort that Pip is only a laborer, she replies, "You can break his heart." Estella proceeds, during the game that follows, to mock Pip's coarse hands, clumsiness, and stupidity. Pip finds her contempt accurate and agrees sadly within himself. To Miss Havisham's questioning, Pip replies that he thinks Estella is proud and insulting and, although she is pretty enough to be worth seeing again, he wants to go home. Pip notices now that everything in the room has stopped dead—that Miss Havisham's unshod foot wears a stocking that is worn to shreds and that the scarcely changing expression on her face is one of deep brooding. It is this lack of change that makes the atmosphere deathly. The game of cards finished, Miss Havisham tells Pip that she knows nothing of time but that he should come back in six days. Estella's candle leads him through the dark corridors, and Pip is surprised to see daylight outside. Alone in the courtyard while Estella goes to get him some lunch, Pip is troubled by his common hands and boots and reminds himself to tell Joe that Jacks should be called Knaves, as Estella has scornfully told him. He wishes he and Joe were genteel. Estella brings his food; setting it before him as though he were a dog. Pausing only long enough to see the tears that her humiliating treatment have brought to Pip's eyes, she leaves again. Alone, Pip cries bitterly behind the gate. This visit, along with the injustices inflicted upon him by his sister, has been too much. After eating his lunch, he feels better and begins to explore the grounds. Wherever he turns, he glimpses Estella disappearing around some far corner or up some stairs. Suddenly, within the brewery, he sees a figure hanging by its neck, dressed in yellowed, aged white. Looking again, he sees it is Miss Havisham but, as he runs toward it in terror, he finds that the hanging figure is not there at all. At last, Estella comes with keys to let him out and, as he goes, she taunts him to go ahead and cry. Pip goes on home; pondering on his own despicable coarseness and ignorance.

COMMENT

Pip's involvement with prisons is clear in his comment about the seeds kept locked up in Mr. Pumblechook's drawers and in his recognition of the attitude toward him shared by Pumblechook and Mrs. Joe. Prisons become an obsessive theme in the chapter for Miss Havisham, in a perverse act of self-punishment, has made her house into a barred prison from which she cannot emerge into the light of day. As a result, her one clear activity is vengeance and Estella is her instrument. This aspect of her life will be developed later in the novel. Like the scene on the marshes in which perception was obscured by the mist, this scene is obscured by the darkness Miss Havisham cherishes. What is presented is vivid and of heightened reality; just because it seems like an illusion. Again, both the convict and Miss Havisham might well be called "flat" characters; that is, characterized by a very few outstanding qualities rather than by a more complex mingling of attributes. Yet, both remain in the reader's imagination and seem, as they must seem to Pip, to be actually larger than life. Such presentations are typical of Dickens' work.

Estella's candle in the dark corridors serves to provide a ghostly quality to the narrative. Pip's comment that her light seems like a star is important. Estella is a name that means "star." The star and Estella's jewel-like beauty, become symbolic of Pip's aspiration for her. Estella's effect on Pip's development will be at least as important as Joe's. We see, in all Pip's descriptions of what he sees, a growing awareness of himself. In this chapter, that awareness increases painfully. To his previous guilt, Pip adds his shame at his own lack of genteel breeding. His new self-consciousness is Pip's first step in the loss of the innocence he has previously shared with Joe. It will have far-reaching effect.

CHAPTER 9

Mrs. Joe has many questions to put to Pip upon his return. Fearing to be misunderstood, Pip gives the shortest possible answers with the result that Mrs. Joe resorts to getting more information by physical pressure. Pip holds back; he is sure that his description of Miss Havisham would not be believed. When Pumblechook arrives full of more curious questions, Pip becomes even more obstinate; especially as Mr. Pumblechook uses arithmetic problems rather than physical force to pry out the answers. Pip finally constructs a fantastic and utterly false account. He describes Miss Havisham as tall and dark, seated in a black velvet coach, and eating cake from golden plates. He also finds himself saying that he and Estella played with flags. They leave Pip alone while they discuss all this. When Joe comes in for tea and the story is related to him Pip is overcome with penitence for Joe is equally amazed and believing. Only toward Joe does Pip feel he has been monstrous in fabricating the account. Mrs. Joe and Pumblechook consider what benefits might come to Pip through this association. Later, Pip joins Joe in the forge and finds courage to confess his lie. Joe is amazed, disappointed, and dismayed at Pip's lie. Pip tries to explain the discomfort he was made to feel by the proud Estella because of his thick boots and coarse hands, but Joe does not think Pip is common. He remarks that Pip is uncommonly small and uncommonly educated and, what is more to the point, that lies are not the way "to get out of being common." Pip insists that he is ignorant and backward to which Joe can only add that perhaps it is best for common men to stick with their kind and not go to play with uncommon ones. He is not angry with Pip but suggests that Pip remember his lie in his prayers and never lie again. Pip does remember, but his mind is so disturbed that he can't help thinking, as he drops off to sleep, how common Estella would find Joe. It has been an important day for him.

COMMENT

Pip's powers of imagination run free in the lie he fabricates and the quality of his imaginings show that he has indeed been affected by his visit. His loyalty to Joe wins out, however, when he confesses his guilt. Thus, the theme of guilt and penitence recurs but, this time, Pip is truly guilty and less repentant than we could hope. His real guilt, as will be stressed later, lies in his newly aroused ambition to be uncommon. It is this that leads to the slight contempt for Joe that lingers in his mind as he falls asleep. The lie and Pip's growing condescension direct his attentions away from Joe's simple (but profoundly true) moral viewpoint and emphasize his first step out of innocence.

CHAPTER 10

Pip realizes that education is a means to becoming less common. At the next session with Mr. Wopsle's great-aunt, he asks Biddy if she will begin to teach him what she knows. Biddy obliges willingly, but the little school is hardly conducive to learning. The room is lighted by one candle, there is only a single spelling book, and the students raise havoc while Mr. Wopsle's great-aunt sleeps the hour away. Biddy's first effort involves reading to Pip from the store's little catalogue and giving him an old-English D to copy. Pip thinks the latter is a design for a belt buckle until he is told otherwise. Pip then goes to meet Joe at the local tavern, the Three Jolly Bargemen; from there, they will walk home together. He finds Joe seated with Mr. Wopsle and a stranger who stares at the boy, nods at him in a furtive manner, and makes room for him to sit beside him. Pip prefers to sit by Joe, and the stranger then nudges him under the table. After buying drinks for all, the stranger turns the conversation cunningly to the surrounding graves and marshes; he wonders whether anyone is ever found thereabouts. Joe recounts briefly the search for the convicts. Then the stranger turns his attention to Pip; inquiring about the boy's name and his relationship to Joe. All the while, he stares at Pip as if taking aim to fire a shot at him. When the shot comes, it is a gesture. The drinks arrive and the man stirs his with a file, in such a way that no one but Pip notices. Immediately, Pip realizes that this man knows his convict. It is time for Pip and Joe to leave and, as they rise, the stranger says he thinks he has a bright new shilling for the boy in his pocket. He takes out some change, wraps it in paper, and gives it to Pip, saying "Mind! Your own." He winks at Pip and they leave. Pip is too confused to talk on the way home and becomes more stunned when they get there and he discovers that the coin is wrapped in two one-pound notes. Joe, believing this to be a mistake, runs back to the tavern with them but the man is gone, as Pip privately expected. Mrs. Joe wraps the notes and puts them in an ornamental teapot where they remain as a nightmarish reminder to Pip. He feels it is "guiltily coarse and common" to be on familiar terms with convicts. He dreams of the file coming at him and wakes up screaming.

COMMENT

Pip is deeply and clearly involved in bettering himself as can be seen from his request to Biddy. His desire to become genteel is even more apparent in his shame at his association with convicts. Facades, or fake exteriors, have become of primary importance to him. Yet, his present state of guilt, as linked with social embarrassment, is as real and full of nightmares as was his more innocent and natural former sense of guilt about stealing the food for the convict. The theme of guilt and punishment has been brought back by the stranger in the tavern, and it reminds us to compare Pip's new reactions to his previous ones.

CHAPTER 11

Pip returns to Miss Havisham on the appointed day and is admitted by Estella who scarcely takes notice of him. She leads him with her candle to a totally different part of the house. Across a courtyard is a smaller house; its clock has also stopped at twenty minutes to nine. Here, Estella takes him to a room with some other people in it and tells him to wait by the window until he is called. The occupants are three ladies and a man, and Pip immediately senses that they are "toadies and humbugs." Everyone seems to be discussing someone else named Matthew; they call him "Poor soul!" and condemn him as having no "sense of the proprieties." One woman, who is named Camilla and reminds Pip of Mrs. Joe, is especially keen on this point. The man, Cousin Raymond and another woman (identified as Sarah Pocket) seem to agree. A bell rings to interrupt the conversation. Pip has been called, and he follows Estella out of the room and back along the passageway. She stops him there and asks if she is pretty and insulting. When he replies yes to the first and no to the second question, Estella slaps Pip's face as hard as she can; she calls him a coarse monster and causes him to cry. Pip vows that he will never cry for her again. As they proceed upstairs, they meet a burly, dark-skinned man who looks closely at Pip and tells him to behave himself. Pip has no idea that this man will come to play an important role in his life. Left at Miss Havisham's room, where nothing has changed, Pip waits until she notices him. When Miss Havisham sees that he is not anxious to play again, she asks if he will work. To this, Pip agrees and is sent into the room across the hall. It, too, is dark and airless; the smoke from the fire there reminds him of the marsh mist. Everything is dusty and decaying. The long center table has been laid for a feast when time stopped in the house; spiders now run to and for along it. Pip is listening to the mice in the walls and watching the beetles on the hearth when Miss Havisham, carrying a cane and looking like a witch, lays her hand on his shoulder. She says that the mound of cobwebs in the middle of the table was her bridal cake and that she will be laid out on this table when she dies. She asks Pip to walk her slowly round and round the table, supporting her hand with his shoulder. Pip calls for Estella and, with Estella, comes the company from downstairs. This makes Pip more uncomfortable than ever. While they talk to Miss Havisham, she and Pip continue to circle the room. When Matthew's name is mentioned again, however, Miss Havisham halts. She declares that she expects Matthew to come when she is dead and to stand at her head when she is laid on this very table. She indicates the places of the others when they shall finally "come to feast upon" her. Then she dismisses them. Miss Havisham tells Pip that today is her birthday and the day she was to have been married. She hopes that she will die on this day. Estella returns and all three stand quietly in the dim room. Pip fears that he and Estella may soon begin to decay along with everything else. They soon return to the other room where he and Estella again play cards. Miss Havisham now shows off Estella's beauty by holding jewels near her breast and hair. Pip is then told when to come back and is fed again like a dog in the courtyard. Wandering about the neglected back garden, Pip sees that a pale young gentleman, a boy about his own age, is there also. Abruptly, he challenges Pip to a fight. Pip agrees. Pip succeeds in laying him out, blow after blow and, each time the young gentleman comes back, until, finally, he is knocked against a wall and admits defeat. He seems so brave and innocent to Pip that Pip considers himself a savage beast. Pip finds Estella, her face flushed with delight, waiting to let him out. As a reward for winning the fight, she allows Pip to kiss her. Although he is glad of the chance, he feels that it has been given like common money and is worthless. He returns to the cottage near the marsh where Joe's forge fire gleams in the darkening afternoon.

COMMENT

Pip senses immediately that the other visitors are "toadies and humbugs" and so they are. Apparently, they all court Miss Havisham for the sake of her money. What Pip doesn't realize is that, in one sense, he is doing so, too. Certainly, Mrs. Joe and Pumblechook consider the advantages of Miss Havisham's property of major importance, and they speculate as to what Pip will get. The relatives have but one morality: propriety, or the facade of manners. They condemn Matthew for lacking this quality. This same facade of manners is gradually becoming Pip's central goal in life. This newly gained attitude is prompted and encouraged by Estella as can be seen clearly in both incidents with her; the slap and the kiss. Pip fails to grasp that Miss Havisham is using him to make her relatives jealous. Pip is an instrument in the hands of the sophisticated, and he is still innocent enough not to understand this. Everything is decay and facade at Miss Havisham's. The two are joined for a purpose. Miss Havisham seems to be enveloped in mist just like the incident on the marshes. It is ironic that Pip's former shame and new aspirations should be so linked.

CHAPTER 12

For the next few days, Pip is pursued by guilt at having fought and beaten the pale young gentleman. He feels sure that country ruffians are not permitted such liberties with gentlefolk, and he feels equally sure that the law will avenge the blood he has shed. He goes so far as to wash out the blood spattered on his trousers; he also keeps an eye out for policemen. When it comes time for him to return to Miss Havisham's, his terrors are at a high pitch. He goes, however, and nothing comes of the fight. A light wheelchair has been obtained by Miss Havisham, and it becomes Pip's duty to push her in it around the house for as long as three hours at a stretch. It is arranged for him to come every other day, and his visits continue for the next ten months. He becomes accustomed to her, and they discuss his plans to be apprenticed to Joe. Pip makes sure that Miss Havisham is aware of his desire to rise, but she seems to prefer him as he is; she never even offers to pay him for his visits. Estella continues to treat Pip badly. Miss Havisham relishes Estella's moods, and encourages her with the words "Break their hearts." The constant wheeling of Miss Havisham's chair, the chanting of a blacksmith song for her entertainment as he does so, the subdued and misty atmosphere of the yellowed rooms . . . all these come to have a deep influence over Pip's gradually maturing spirit during these months. Pip becomes secretive about the visits. He even neglects to tell Joe about the fight and confides only in Biddy.

Every night, Pumblechook and Mrs. Joe hash over Pip's prospects with respect to Miss Havisham. Joe sits silently saddened at the prospect of losing Pip as his apprentice. One day, however, Miss Havisham instructs Pip to bring Joe to her with the papers that will make Pip Joe's apprentice. When Pip relays this message, Mrs. Joe goes on a bigger Rampage than ever.

COMMENT

Clearly, Pip has expectations with regard to Miss Havisham and his future. He does his best to intimate as much to the lady but with no results. He serves only one purpose; he is an object through which Miss Havisham takes revenge on mankind through Estella. Possibly, she does not even realize that the atmosphere around him evokes Pip's desires for a "better" life. She is too single-minded in her revenge to think of consequences. Along with his expectations, Pip conceives a growing dislike for the vulgar frankness of Mrs. Joe's hopes along that line. Pip has many conflicts, but the theme of his own hopes for property and position is obvious here.

CHAPTER 13

The next day, Joe dresses in his Sunday suit. Pip is saddened by Joe's efforts to look well and by his own awareness that Joe looks worse. Mrs. Joe, wearing all of her "articles of property," comes along. She plans to stay at Mr. Pumblechook's during the visit. Pip and an uncomfortable Joe are conducted to Miss Havisham by Estella; she ignores them as always. Joe proves so ill at ease upon meeting Miss Havisham that he cannot speak to her; he addresses all his remarks to Pip. He explains that he felt Pip's apprenticeship would lead "to larks." Pip feels ashamed of Joe's manner of addressing him instead of Miss Havisham. He sees Estella laughing when Joe removes the papers from his hat and says that, of course, no premium or money is expected. Pip does notice, however, that Miss Havisham looks with understanding on the simple man. She picks up a bag and gives it to Joe. The bag contains twenty-five guineas which Pip has earned. Miss Havisham makes it clear that no other or further reward is to be expected from her. Joe, who seems out of his mind with wonder, thanks Pip profusely. Pip learns from Miss Havisham that Joe is now his master and that he should come to her no more. They depart and, once outside the gate, the overwhelmed blacksmith can only murmur "astonishing." They head for Pumblechook's where Mrs. Joe is waiting. Joe recounts two falsehoods there: first, he conveys Miss Havisham's compliments to Mrs. J. Gargery; second, he presents the money as a gift from Miss Havisham to her. Pumblechook, "the abject hypocrite," pretends that he knew it all along and, grabbing Pip in the most patronizing way, insists on overseeing the ceremony of the boy's being bound as apprentice. His manner of escorting Pip to the court is such that onlookers assume the boy has been taken for a crime. Then, the group goes to dinner at the Blue Boar to celebrate, and Pip is miserable and wretched throughout. Upon arriving home, he sadly feels that, although he had liked Joe's trade once, he does not now and never will again.

COMMENT

Joe has so little sense of property that he regards even the pie, which he believed Pip's convict stole, as Mrs. Joe's rather than as his own. However, Mrs. Joe's sense of property is her religion (as can be seen in this and preceding scenes). Pumblechook, who has by now been characterized as very pompous and moralistic, is equally pompous and patronizing in his attitude toward the newly received property. His remarks, which formerly centered on Pip's ingratitude, now center on the word "bound." Pip is bound as an apprentice to Joe and, while the trade does not imprison the blacksmith, it does prove very confining to Pip because of his loss of innocence and his newly conceived expectations. Bondage has been important as an imposed punishment for the convict and as the self-imposed affliction of Miss Havisham. Pip has been bound up in his relations with Joe by his guilt and by his hopes; these have been instilled by Miss Havisham and by Estella. His bondage is now far more complete and seems to place an insurmountable obstacle between himself and the life he desires. The Hall of Justice, where this formal binding takes place, reinforces Pip's psychological perception of being taken into prison. Even the bystanders sense this and jeer. It is ironical that the property, for which Pip secretly hoped, proves to be akin to a prisoner's chain when it comes; hampering his movement up the social scale. The theme of property has been stressed here, and it is property that uses the possessor rather than being used by him.

Official justice, of which Pumblechook has thus far been the self-appointed administrator, shows itself to be self-important and ridiculous at the Hall of Justice. Dickens often treated it so, notably in *Bleak House*. It is also worth noting that even the egotistical Miss Havisham perceives Joe's dignity at the very moment when Pip is feeling most ashamed of his friend. Joe is a completely sympathetic character, and his indirect manner of addressing Miss Havisham communicates more completely his goodness than any facade of social ease. His total lack of facade wins Miss Havisham and embarrasses Pip who has begun to seek such a facade. Pip is lowered a bit in our estimation because of it; at the same time, Miss Havisham rises thanks to her understanding. The visit, however, subtly conveys a certain facade to Joe and, for the sake of preserving peace, he is capable, upon returning to Mrs. Joe, of a very tactful lie.

CHAPTER 14

For Pip, Joe had always made their cottage pleasant. The parlor had seemed elegant, and the forge has been a road to manhood. Now, through his own weakness (and his exposure to Mrs. Joe and Miss Havisham), Pip has reached the miserable state of feeling ashamed of his home. The road to freedom, through the forge, now seems like a road to slavery and he faces it with "dull endurance." His future seems as low, flat, and full of dark mists as the marshes. Happily, Pip never makes the slightest mention of this to Joe. Pip feels strongly that whatever good was in himself at that time came from "plain, contented Joe;" rather than from "restless, aspiring, discontented me." Pip does not know what he wants. He only knows that he is afraid that someday, when he is covered with coal dust and at his most common, Estella's face will appear to exult over him and despise him. Gradually and ironically, he becomes guilty of ingratitude to those who have been bringing him up; a sin of which he has always been accused.

COMMENT

The chapter is a straightforward one. It gives direct expression to Pip's aspirations and his sense of shame, the guilt that goes with these, and his feelings of imprisonment. All are thematically central to the narrative.

CHAPTER 15

Pip has grown too old for the school of Mr. Wopsle's great-aunt and has learned everything that Biddy can teach him. He accepts everything gravely. He even asks Mr. Wopsle to instruct him further, but he quits after serving as audience and being mauled in one of Mr. Wopsle's poetic furies. Pip tries to teach Joe what he knows; with an eye to making the blacksmith less ignorant, less common, and less open to Estella's reproach. Joe takes the lessons with a pleased air of increasing wisdom, but he never succeeds in learning anything. The studies are held on the marshes on Sundays. The clouds, the green hills, and the sails of ships constantly remind Pip of Miss Havisham and Estella and their equally picturesque life. Finally, one afternoon, he mentions to Joe that he wishes to visit Miss Havisham again. Joe discourages this because he thinks that she might take Pip's visit as a sign that he expected more from her. Joe reminds Pip how Miss Havisham said that there would be no more payment of any kind to him. He feels that she meant, by this, that Pip should keep his distance. Although Pip acknowledges this within himself, he persists and says that he has never properly thanked Miss Havisham. Pip persists in wishing to make the visit and, and Joe is not one to oppose him. He insists, however, that this trip be the last unless it is greeted with great encouragement. Joe has a helper at the forge, a swarthy and very strong fellow named Orlick who slouches to and from work with his eyes on the ground. Orlick suspects that Pip will replace him, and he harbors much hostility against the boy. When he hears that Pip is to be allowed the afternoon off, he insists on being let off also. Upon hearing this, Mrs. Joe works herself into a rage. When Orlick retorts that she is a "foul shrew," she forces herself into a violently furious state. Briefly, Orlick describes the choking Mrs. Joe would get if she were his wife. Since Mrs. Joe's temper results in a dramatic fit, Joe finds it necessary to challenge Orlick's remarks. A fight ensues during which Orlick is knocked insensible. When Pip returns from changing his clothes, Mrs. Joe is calm and Joe is sharing a pot of beer with Orlick. Pip's visit with Miss Havisham is short. In response to her sharp question, he answers that he does not want anything but has only come to thank her. She softens and tells him to visit her on his birthday from now on. Seeing him glance around for Estella, Miss Havisham tells him with malignant enjoyment that the girl is abroad; being educated as a lady. The visit over, Pip wanders through town. There, he meets Mr. Wopsle who insists on taking the boy to one of his dramatic readings at Pumblechook's. Pip liistens to the reading during which Pumblechook intones "Take warning" at Pip during one tragic scene. On the way home with Mr. Wopsle, they meet Orlick who tells them that he, too, has been in town and has heard cannons fired from the prison ships, which means escaped convicts. Passing the pub, they learn that the Gargery household has been broken into and that someone there has been hurt. Arriving at a run, Pip finds the cottage full of people. Lying on the floor is Mrs. Joe; knocked sense-less by a tremendous blow on the head.

COMMENT

The chapter full of foreboding or doom. Joe's attitude toward the visit to Miss Havisham's is based upon his apprehension that no good can come of it. Miss Havisham herself is malicious in her desire to see Pip suffer over the unattainability of Estella. The fight between Joe and Orlick brings a shudder (despite its peaceful conclu-sion) because of Orlick's personal effect on us as a man of evil tendencies. Pip's response to Pumblechook's "Take warning" is full of guilt. On the way home, Orlick's appearance out of the mist and his remark about the cannons form a vague link between him and the threat-ening younger convict on the marshes. The forebodings here extend to the entire sequence of the narrative and to Pip's future but, for the moment, they culminate in calamity: the frightful attack on and serious injury of Mrs. Joe. Pip's aspirations and guilty shame are related both to vague prophecies and to the present insistence of evil.

CHAPTER 16

Pip's intense dislike for his sister, his ingrained sense of guilt, and his recent experience at Pumblechook's tragic reading all conspire to make him feel that, somehow, he has had a hand in the attack on Mrs. Joe and that he also falls under suspi-cion. However he soon relieves himself of the feeling. Evidence shows that Mrs. Joe had been standing with her face to the fire when someone entered the house and struck her on the back of the head with a convict's leg-iron. The iron does not belong to either of the recently escaped convicts and was, in fact, filed apart some time ago. Pip feels sure it is his convict's old iron. He suspects one of two people: the man with the file or Orlick (who lives on the dark marsh and might well have found the iron). Yet, there could be no motive for the man with the file: his two pounds had been kept for him and there was no conversation between Mrs. Joe and her assailant. As for Orlick, his statement that he had been in town was supported by numerous witnesses. Pip feels horrible to think he had supplied the weapon but, whenever he wishes to make a clean breast of it to Joe, he decides against it. His secret is old and ingrown and he fears to alienate Joe. Mrs. Joe's sight, her hearing, speech, and her memory are all impaired. She can only communicate by writing on a slate that her temper and patience are much improved. Biddy comes to take care of her and proves a blessing all around, especially to the saddened Joe. Mrs. Joe often draws a sign that looks like a hammer and then signifies a desire for it. It is Biddy who finally solves the mystery, and she brings Orlick to Mrs. Joe. The disabled woman is at last satisfied. She receives Orlick with all evidences of humble conciliation and concern that he be pleased with his reception. Soon, this begins to occur daily. Orlick always stands before Mrs. Joe as though he does not know what to make of it. Nor does Pip.

COMMENT

Pip's guilt, and his inability to confide it and so relieve himself, are evident here. He remains too concerned about the judgment of others to tell Joe his secret, so he clings to insincerity. Biddy's quickness of understanding is emphasized and, for the rest of the chapter, there is an atmosphere of gloom, and the plot thickens. Orlick is linked with the threatening marshes, but Mrs. Joe's behavior to him does away with suspicion.

CHAPTER 17

Pip's life now falls into a routine that includes visiting Miss Havisham on his birthday. Estella remains absent, and Miss Havisham's remarks about her to Pip are always the same. Each year she gives him a guinea for his birthday present. The timeless and yellowed room continues to exert its influence on Pip making him dissatisfied and ashamed. Biddy, however, becomes brighter and prettier. Her wholesomeness and her good, attentive eyes make their impression on Pip. He observes, however, that she is not beautiful like Estella; for she is common. Pip spends his birthday pocket money on books and becomes a bit vain about his knowledge. Still, he admires Biddy's own degree of learning and is impressed that she seems to "catch it—like a cough," rather than work for it. Again, he admires how she has made the most of every chance and risen so far above her original circumstances with Mr. Wopsle's great-aunt. When Pip tells Biddy how extraordinary she seems to him, he brings tears to her eyes. This prompts Pip to realize that he has not been sufficiently grateful to her. He decides to confide in Biddy more and asks her to take a walk with him on the marshes on Sunday. It is summer and, as they walk, Pip once more connects the green hills and white sails with Estella and Miss Havisham. He confides to Biddy that he wants to be a gentleman. He tells her how miserable he is with his present life and, while Biddy believes that he will be more so as a gentleman, she does not want Pip to be unhappy. He agrees that it is a pity that he cannot settle down to be half as fond of the forge as he was in childhood. He wishes Estella had never told him he was coarse and common. Then, confessing his admiration for Estella's beauty, Pip falls to tearing at the grass. Biddy asks him if he wants to be a gentleman to spite Estella or if he wants to gain her over. She observes mildly that spite would be more independent of Pip. She adds that she does not think such a lady is worth gaining over. Pip admits all this is true but he cannot help admiring Estella anyway. Fully knowing the madness at his heart, Pip now tears at his hair and wishes to punish himself. Biddy stops trying to reason with him. She comforts him and wishes he were not beyond the lesson she could teach him now. Everything Biddy says seems right to Pip but, when he says that he wishes he would fall in love with her, she answers that she is sure he never shall. The pair are interrupted by Orlick who appears out of the mud and rushes. He insists on accompanying them, but Biddy whispers her protests to Pip. Orlick drops back with a laugh but follows at a distance. Biddy explains that she dislikes Orlick because he seems to like her, whereupon Pip resolves to keep himself between Orlick and the girl—much to the Orlick's vengeful annoyance. Thereafter, Pip falls into a complete confusion; wavering between his sense of the goodness in Biddy and Joe and the honest life they represent; and in his hopes, through Miss Havisham, for property, social position, and, perhaps, even Estella.

COMMENT

The chapter deals with the division between Miss Havisham's life and Joe's and between Estella and Biddy. Throughout, the two alternatives appear in comparison. Biddy's warmth of feeling and true wisdom is much like Joe's and has the same simple dignity. Clearly, Dickens approves of this honest plain way of life, and even Pip has gained the maturity to appreciate it. However, education remains his goal, and he even becomes vain about it. His decision to confide in Biddy is self-serving, and his confession to her is unintentionally cruel. He lacks her insight into people and fails to notice what she feels for him. Just as the narrative moves between the truth in Joe's way of life and the cruel superficiality represented by Miss Havisham's way, Pip's thoughts and attitudes bound and rebound between them. Yet, he remains so impressed with the larger-than-life, illusory magnificence of Satis House that he fails to see it realistically. For Pip, it remains a romance to be hoped for.

CHAPTER 18

It is a Saturday night in Pip's fourth year of apprenticeship and he and Joe sit in the Three Jolly Bargemen. They are listening to Mr. Wopsle's rendition of a recently committed murder. A contemptuous stranger speaks out and, with distinct authority, grills Mr. Wopsle on his right to judge the accused as guilty. The stranger argues with a firm knowledge of the law and shows up Mr. Wopsle as a fool. Settling back, he then asks aloud to the room for Joe Gargery, the black-smith, and for his apprentice, Pip. Immediately, Pip recognizes him as the man who stopped him on the stairs at Miss Havisham's house. This man has a message to give Pip in private, and he requests that they go to Joe's cottage. The walk is silent, and Joe uses the front door and the parlor (an acknowledgment that he is impressed). The man introduces himself as Jaggers, a London lawyer, who has come as the confidential agent of another person. Jaggers proceeds to ask Joe if he would object, or ask for money, if he were requested to give up his apprentice and cancel the binding papers. Joe, who would never stand in Pip's way, stares hard and says firmly, "No." Jaggers seems to think this foolish on Joe's part, but he turns to deliver his message to Pip saying, "He has Great Expectations." Over his own gasps, Pip hears that he has come into valuable property and that its giver wishes him to brought up as a gentleman. This is a reality beyond Pip's wildest dreams, and he is sure that Miss Havisham is providing a grand fortune for him. There are two stipulations to which Pip immediately agrees. First, he is always to go by the name of Pip. Second, he will not be told the name of his benefactor until that person reveals it personally in the indefinite future. He is not to inquire into, refer to, or even make guesses as to the person's identity. Jaggers will be his guardian and will dispense money to him and arrange for his education. He feels that a certain Matthew Pocket would be a suitable tutor and, at Pip's expression of recognition (surely this is the Matthew that Miss Havisham and her relatives spoke about), Jaggers asks him what he has to say. Pip agrees to try Mr. Pocket, and to come to London immediately to begin his education. Turning to Joe, Jaggers wonders how Joe would feel about receiving a present of money in compensation for the loss of Pip's services. At this, good Joe breaks down and says that money cannot compensate for the loss of Pip. Jaggers makes one more offer of money which is refused. To Pip's pointed question as to whether he may take leave of uptown friends (meaning Miss Havisham), Jaggers shrugs "yes" and goes. Pip tells Biddy of his good fortune, and both she and Joe congratulate him. He, on the other hand, resents the touch of sadness in their words and the degree of their wonder at his becoming a gentleman. Biddy does her best to convey the news to Pip's sister but that lady's mind is so darkened that even this, which would have meant so much to her before, is beyond her understanding. As Joe and Biddy cheer up and relax, Pip becomes more gloomy and, years later, as he narrates the story, he realizes that even then he must have been dissatisfied with his own behavior (without having recognized it). Although he has no reason to be so, Pip is offended by what he feels is their mistrust. Even the stars that night seem poor and humble to Pip. He makes plans to go to the tailor for new clothes. Biddy suggests that Pip show himself to his sister, Joe, and her before leaving for London. With an air of forgiving her for implying that he would do otherwise, Pip agrees. He retires with some mixed emotions about his good fortune.

COMMENT

In the scene after Mr. Wopsle has read the murder account and pronounced the accused guilty, Jaggers proceeds to make everyone feel guilty, especially Wopsle. The blunt spoken lawyer has this capacity and even makes Pip feel as though he knows much that would shame the boy. However, Pip's situation is full of many budding feelings and a careful distinction must be made between Pip as a child and Pip as adult narrator. The narrator condemns Pip across the distance of years and holds him accountable for a real failure when he denies his own sense of obligation, love, and guilt so that his new fortune not be tarnished by sadness or guilty feelings. From this point of view, he resents the slightest indication from Joe and Biddy that he should feel sad. Biddy sees through Pip and can annoy him by pinpointing his lack of human response. Joe, who has always had an aura of sanctity for the boy, just blesses him uncritically. Still, the false pride that envelops Pip so promptly (and his refusal to admit his own feelings) isolates him quickly from Joe and Biddy. He is alienated from them by his own failings. These are failings that emerge with his acquisition of property and the realization of his hopes. Pip immediately settles on Miss Havisham as his benefactress and begins to adopt a social facade of denying his own responses. Property is using Pip rather than the reverse, and Pip starts by letting property replace people. Such a thing could never happen to Joe, as the blacksmith indicates clearly to the departing Jaggers. For Pip, however, all is aspiration. Property and guilt are linked for him but he chooses to ignore the latter.

CHAPTER 19

Pip wakes up cheerful and anxious for the six days' wait before his departure to be over. At breakfast, Joe brings out the apprenticeship papers and he and Pip burn them together. Feeling very free, Pip goes to church; there, he cannot believe the preacher's story of how difficult it is for a rich man to enter into heaven. The church makes him feel compassion for the people who will attend it for a dreary succession of Sundays until they are buried there. He remembers, with shame, his wretched convict and is comforted to think that the incident is long past. After church, Pip falls asleep on the marsh. He wakes to find Joe who has come to keep him company. Joe has thought things over and seems sure in his knowledge that Pip will not forget their friendship. This bothers Pip for he feels that Joe should be more grateful at the idea of the new gentleman. However, he says nothing about this to Joe. Pip tells Joe that he wishes that he were better educated and later Pip mentions this to Biddy and suggests that she help Joe with learning and manners. In her quiet way, Biddy is incensed. She points out that Joe is too proud to allow anyone to lift him from a place that he fills well and with respect. Pip brushes this remark off disdainfully as evidence of Biddy's envy. He tells her so; in a "virtuous and superior tone." Biddy answers that a gentleman has no more right to be unjust than a plain man. Pip's second night of fortune is as lonely as the first. He does not mention the matter again next morning but goes to see Mr. Trabb, the tailor. Trabb greets him warmly but becomes more distant and respectful upon learning of Pip's new fortune and his desire for a suit of clothes. Trabb's boy, however, sweeps over Pip's shoes and knocks his broom about as if to affirm his equality with Pip. Trabb takes Pip's measurements. The suit will be sent to Pumblechook's on Thursday. Feeling satisfied, Pip buys hats, boots, socks, and his ticket to London, explaining his new fortune everywhere. He then goes to Pumblechook's where Pumblechook fawns in the manner Pip feels is due him and, apparently, shares Pip's belief that Miss Havisham is the benefactress. He serves Pip an elegant meal, quite unlike the breakfast of Pip's first visit, and punctuates the meal with fervent requests to shake Pip's hand. After considerable toasting, Pip becomes convinced, by wine and Pumblechook's servility, that he has previously been mistaken about that fine fellow. Pumblechook even offers him a partnership in his seed business, in exchange for an outlay of capital. Pip decides to wait on that and takes his leave, only to have Pumblechook chase after him for a last handshake. Days pass and Pip returns to the seed merchant to try on his suit. Pumblechook is not home so, after dressing, Pip decides to go to Miss Havisham's. Sarah Pocket admits him. Miss Havisham has heard of Pip's good fortune from Jaggers and she congratulates him as though she were a fairy godmother. She makes sure to do this in the presence of the envious Sarah Pocket and seems to accept Pip's hesitant gratitude. She makes a gloating show of the fact that she knows the details about the anonymous benefactor. She says goodbye and Pip kneels to this triumphant, weird woman who brandishes her crutch like a wand. A confounded Sarah lets him out. Pip then changes his clothes at Pumblechook's and heads home. The days have passed quickly, Pip again puts on his new clothes and sits down to a sumptuous but low-spirited last dinner with Biddy and Joe. Alone in his room, Pip admits to himself that the reason he has requested to walk alone to the village the next morning is his consciousness of Joe's awkwardness beside him. Pip has an impulse to ask Joe to accompany him after all, but he does not. He dreams of journeys which fail. Pip wakes to the smell of Biddy's cooking and, after some hesitation, goes down. Breakfast is tasteless. Good-byes are a bit brisk and short. Pip's last view as he goes off down the road is of Joe and Biddy, calling to him through their tears, and throwing old shoes after him. Pip whistles and makes light of departing, glad to have avoided shoes thrown publicly at the coach he will board. Light mists rise, and at the end of the village, Pip breaks into sobs and says a real good-bye to his dear friend Joe. He is better then—sadder, gentler, more aware of his own ingratitude. Once on the coach, he even considers getting off and walking back for the sake of a better parting, but he never does.

COMMENT

Pip has distinctly emerged from what one critic calls the innocence of Eden. At the end of the chapter, he leaves the pastoral and rural setting of his youth with its mists. The mist clears away from his heart as well as from the landscape, and Pip is left with the hard light of reality showing him the world with the experience and expectation it holds for him. In the course of the chapter, Pip's growing experience and rising expectations do not show him in a pleasant light. His exhibits pride and falsely virtuous attitudes. He considers himself above the preacher's warnings about wealth; the thought of his convict leaves him ashamed. Pip has lost the sense of guilt and ingratitude that were part of his innocence. He ignores his instinctive human responses; repressing them until he is reluctant to face the love of Joe and Biddy. Instead, Pip revels in fanciful thoughts about his future and relishes the power of money over townspeople such as Trabb. He has lost the acute perception of his youth to such an extent that Pumblechook's clearly greedy bootlicking does not offend him. Having lost this human insight, Pip fails to take notice of how Miss Havisham allows herself to be mistaken for his benefactress in order to torment Sarah Pocket. He unconsciously permits himself to be deceived. He is no longer the morally outcast orphan victimized by the provincial morality of Mrs. Joe and her friends. His innocence was first broken by the shame, instilled by Estella. Desire not to be ashamed led Pip to the hope of acquiring a gentleman's facade. This could only be accomplished with money and, thanks to the discussions of Mrs. Joe and Pumblechook, Pip's hopes focused on Miss Havisham. Pip desires Estella's love in the same way that he desires property. Now that the property has come, Pip casts off shame, guilt, and any indebtedness to Joe. Pride of a very unattractive nature emerges to replace these other emotions. In this last chapter of Stage One, Pip's pride and newly assumed facade are contrasted emphatically with the honest and humble feelings found in Biddy and Joe. For all his dignified appearance, Pip retains none of their native innocence, or innate dignity.

STAGE TWO

CHAPTER 20

The journey to London takes five hours. London frightens Pip with its size, and he chooses to ignore the ugliness and filth he sees there. He hires a ragged hackney-coach that takes him to Jaggers' door; which the coachman appears to know and fear. Inside, Jaggers has left word that Pip should wait in his office until he returns. In a room lighted only by a sky-light, Pip contemplates a rusty pistol, two plaster casts of peculiarly swollen faces, and Jaggers' coffinlike chair. He grows rapidly more depressed and, finally, he leaves for a short walk around the neighborhood. The area, however, is oppressive and filthy. He finds Newgate Prison where a drunken jailer shows him the gallows. Pip's impression of London is a sickening one. Strolling further, Pip discovers others walking; they are also waiting for Jaggers. He soon appears and everyone rushes toward him. Taking Pip with him, the lawyer walks on; interviewing other clients as he goes, telling a woman her Bill is in good hands, and asking if Wemmick has been paid. Jaggers dismisses another person. At his office, a one-eyed man named Mike reports that he has found a witness who will swear to anything. Mike receives a stern reproval and is told to bring the man, who is dressed like a pastry-cook, past the window. The witness proves to be murderous-looking, and Jaggers refuses to have anything to do with him. This business ended, Jaggers tells Pip he is to stay with young Herbert Pocket in his rooms at Barnard's Inn until the next Monday. Then the two will go to Matthew Pocket's where Pip will study if it suits him. Pip's allowance is liberal, and Jaggers adds that he will attempt to keep Pip out of debt and from going wrong.

COMMENT

London filth is more than a match for the fogs on the marsh, and Dickens' depiction of that city is not pleasant. On his very first day, Pip is exposed to the menacing prison and the depravity and evil of the surrounding area. Jaggers is clearly a popular lawyer, not above the most underhanded and illegal tricks. However, he always maintains a hypocritical facade that will allow no admission of these tricks. So far, Pip's visit has been most depressing, and Pip finds himself somewhat bewildered. The theme of crime and criminals reappears.

CHAPTER 21

Pip observes Wemmick, the clerk, as they walk. He sees a dry little man with a square wooden face and frayed linen (indicating bachelorhood). He is laden with tokens of mourning but his eyes glitter keenly. The two talk of London. Wemmick describes it as a good place in which to get cheated, robbed, or murdered. He tells Pip that he knows Matthew Pocket and does not have a high opinion of him. Pip is despressed. His spirits sink even lower at the sight of Barnard's Inn, a bunch of dingy, shabby buildings. Wemmick misinterprets Pip's dismay as a sign that the place is too countrified. He takes Pip to the proper door where he is to wait for the younger Pocket's return and goes his way. Pip waits about a half-hour until the form of a person about his own age rises into view up the stairway. Pocket, Jr. struggles with the door and, all the while, Pip stares as if in a dream. The young man talks on about the arrangement of their quarters until he catches Pip's stare. Both fall back in cries of recognition. This person is none other than the pale young gentleman with whom he had once fought.

COMMENT

The mechanical aspect of Wemmick does little to introduce any human element into Pip's first view of London. The inn confirms the impression of the city as a place of death, decay, and sorrow; it seems to be of that character itself. Dickens' description foreshadows Joe's impression of the inn as a place not fit to keep a pig in, if you wanted that pig to grow fat and healthy. In these deathly surroundings, the pale young gentleman seems to Pip like a ghost of the past.

CHAPTER 22

Pip and the pale young gentleman stare, exclaim, and laugh. Herbert Pocket apologizes for having beaten Pip and, rather than argue, Pip replies modestly. They shake hands warmly. Herbert explains that Miss Havisham had invited him that day to see if she liked him. If she had, Herbert would have been provided for and also engaged to Estella. However, Miss Havisham did not like Herbert, and he is just as glad, for he finds Estella hard and cold. He tells Pip that Estella was adopted and raised by Miss Havisham to take vengeance on the male sex. All this is news to Pip, so Herbert promises to explain everything over supper. Jaggers is Pip's guardian and Miss Havisham's lawyer, and Herbert's father is Miss Havisham's cousin although he is out of her good graces because he will not pay court to her. These are the links that have brought Pip and Herbert together. Pip likes Herbert's frank and easy manner and feels that he could never be secret or mean. At the same time, Pip feels sure that he will never be rich or successful. Still, Pip cannot but observe that his new friend's old clothes are more becoming than Pip's new ones. He responds to Herbert's lack of reserve by relating his own story and even asks that Herbert correct his manners. Herbert decides to call Pip "Handel" because of that composer's piece of music, "The Harmonious Blacksmith." Dinner arrives and Pip enjoys the feeling of eating a good meal without the company of elders. Over dinner, Herbert tells Miss Havisham's story. She was raised by a father who indulged her badly and who had a son by his cook. This son turned out poorly; being riotous and extravagant. When the old man died, he left the larger portion of his estate to Miss Havisham. As a beautiful heiress, she was much courted. Her brother meanwhile ran himself slowly into debt and harbored a grudge against her. A showy man, by no means a gentleman, began to court Miss Havisham and she fell passionately in love. He used her affections to get money from her and persuaded her to buy out her brother's share in the brewery for a very high price. At this point, Matthew Pocket warned Miss Havisham about her lover's conniving. She ordered him out and he never returned. A wedding day was fixed and everything arranged but, on that day, a letter arrived from the bridegroom, heartlessly breaking off the marriage. He then shared the brother's profits. When Miss Havisham recovered from her initial shock, she laid the house to waste and never saw daylight again. This is all Herbert knows. Pip senses that Herbert too feels that Miss Havisham must be his benefactor. He also learns that Herbert has great dreams of financial success, but is now working in a counting house. He bears his poverty, Pip notes, as well as he bore his defeat in the garden. The two soon begin to amuse themselves at the theater and in the parks. Even as Pip wishes it were Joe's job to shoe all the horses in the parks, he senses that a great geographical and social distance has come between him and his dear blacksmith. Yet he still feels twinges of guilt on thinking of the old cottage and his behavior. On Monday, Pip sets out with Herbert for the house of Matthew Pocket in Hammersmith. The little garden there is filled with children, who seem to be tumbling up rather than growing. Mrs. Pocket, who is reading under a tree, greets Pip amiably. Two nurses, Flopson and Millers, chase after the six children and tend to Mrs. Pocket. Matthew Pocket, a man with a perplexed expression on his face and wild gray hair, comes to greet Pip.

COMMENT

This chapter has done much to forward the plot. Miss Havisham's story is at last fully revealed. Her property was the source of her lover's affection and of her own tragedy. Her peculiar existence and her desire for revenge have their motives. Pip's own property, and Herbert's hopes for some, are treated. Both young men have expectations, though Herbert's are grounded more in fantasy than in concrete opportunity. Property and expectations, however, are not the only themes treated. Pip's overbearing pride is still evident in his underlying hope that Herbert will not become rich or successful, in his faintly envious observation of Herbert's manner of wearing clothes and eating dinner, and in his relief to learn that Herbert's schemes are still only dreams. Herbert is Pip's social equal and since he is amiable as well, Pip enjoys his company and does not display his own sense of pride. The amusingly abstracted Mrs. Pocket, her tumbling household, and the confused Matthew Pocket, are introduced.

CHAPTER 23

Matthew Pocket greets Pip with genuine warmth. He is young-looking, natural, and, yet, forever comically upset and confused. Pip soon learns that Mrs. Pocket is the only daughter of a rather vague and unsure line of nobility. She was brought up to marry a title and guarded from "plebian domestic knowledge." She became "highly ornamental, but perfectly helpless and useless." Pip is taken to his pleasant room and introduced to two other students: Bentley Drummle, a heavy-set, old-looking young man who is heir to a title, and Startop, who seems younger and more studious. Pip learns that Mr. Pocket had distinguished himself at Cambridge, married, and failing in loftier hopes, had come to London and taken up tutoring. The aristocratic disposition of Mrs. Pocket requires more than Mr. Pocket can give. Mrs. Pocket's single interest is the nobility, which she discusses over dinner with the sulky Drummle. When a servant finally arrives with the news that the beef is mislaid, Mr. Pocket can bear no more. He amazes Pip with his efforts to lift himself out of his seat by pulling his own hair. The children are brought in afterward, and Mrs. Pocket, who has no idea how to play with them, disregards the baby in her lap to converse with Drummle. When Jane, an adult little girl, finally saves the infant from poking its eyes out with a nutcracker, Mrs. Pocket scolds her with a great show of dignity. The result of this is a small argument with her husband. Peace is awkwardly restored when he attempts again to lift himself by the hair. That evening, Pip rows out on the river with Drummle and Startop. Upon returning home, yet another domestic upset disturbs the peace. After this, Pip retires.

COMMENT

Dickens' depiction of Mrs. Pocket borders on farce but, considered carefully, it is a denunciation of all she stands for. She is a woman devoid of even basic responses to her own children. She has given up such human activity entirely for the sake of a frivolous, vain, and ego-boosting pose as a lady of noble blood. Hers is a sin of pride. She also has little regard for human values. Both these traits may be found, less exaggerated, in Pip. The themes of pride, appearances, and desire for social position are shown in a new and satirical light.

CHAPTER 24

Mr. Pocket speaks to Pip about his education and reveals that Pip is not to be educated for any specific profession. He promises to do all in his power to help Pip, and, in return for this admirable man's zeal as a tutor, Pip does him justice as a pupil. Their relationship proves to be a fine one. With a view to varying his life and improving his manners, Pip decides to keep his room at Herbert's apartment in Barnard's Inn and visits Jaggers to discuss the plan. Jaggers agrees, and after a rather disagreeable discussion as to how much should be paid for furniture, Wemmick is ordered to give Pip twenty pounds. Commenting on Jaggers' manner, Pip learns from Wemmick that the unhumorous, sinister behavior of Jaggers is his professional way; and is actually part of the reason for his success. Wemmick is feeling talkative. He explains that the two grisly plaster casts in Jaggers' office are taken from two of their clients, after they had come down from the gallows. One had murdered his master, and the other had forged checks. Wemmick has an ornamental pin given him by the former and a ring from the latter. His motto is, "Get hold of portable property." Wemmick has warmed up considerably and now invites Pip to visit him at his home in Walworth. Pip accepts.

Wemmick also tells Pip that he will be invited to dine with Jaggers sometimes. When he is, Pip should take particular notice of the housekeeper, who is a wild beast tamed by Jaggers' peculiar power. Wemmick and Pip now go out to see Jaggers "at it." The lawyer is in court and is putting everybody there (including the judge) through the mill to such an extent that they are shrinking and trembling in dread before him.

COMMENT

Clearly, Jaggers' business is to defend the guilty. The lawyer has a tremendous grasp of basic human guilt. We have seen this in his professional ability to make all men, Pip included, feel guilty. It is a power which extends over the judges themselves and is probably the greatest factor in Jaggers' success. The theme of criminals begins to take on larger meaning. Dickens uses Jaggers to make the point that every man senses some criminal guilt within himself. If guilt is one motivating force in human beings, property is another. In the case of men who forge checks, desire for property becomes the motivation for crime. In Pip's case, the receipt of property has caused his very guilty behavior towards Biddy and Joe. Property emerges here as a basic underlying force in even the wooden-faced Wemmick, as his motto reveals.

CHAPTER 25

Pip makes it his custom to spend some evenings rowing on the river with his fellow students, Startop and Bentley Drummle. Often, as he and Startop move their boats homeward down a path of sunlight or moonlight in the center of the river, they see the sulky, arrogant, and suspicious Drummle rowing after them in the still, dark waters by the bank. On one occasion, the Pocket home is paid a visit by Miss Havisham's other relatives: Camilla, her husband, and the rigid Georgiana. Although they are resentful and greedy about Pip's good fortune, they fawn upon him. Pip settles down now to his serious education and his frivolous and expensive habits. Yet, with Herbert as his friend, and Mr. Pocket as his tutor, he manages well. Pip agrees to spend one evening with Wemmick at his home in Walworth. They meet at Jaggers' office and walk there together. Wemmick describes their coming supper and tells Pip to expect an invitation from Jaggers soon. He adds that Jaggers never locks his own house at night; so frightened would any thief be at the thought of robbing him. The pair soon arrive at Wemmick's home. It is a tiny wooden cottage with fake gothic windows and the top cut and painted to look like a castle battlement. A deep ditch separates the garden from the street and, with great pride, Wemmick hauls up a little plank drawbridge after they have crossed. At the back are pigs, goats, and a vegetable garden so that, if the castle were besieged, it would not lack provisions. Wemmick has done all the work himself and shows it with pleasure; explaining that it helps to brush the cobwebs of Newgate Prison away. Inside the castle, Pip is introduced to the well-cared-for, cheerful, but totally deaf old man who is Wemmick's Aged Parent. The Aged P. is most pleased when visitors nod at him and Pip complies. Wemmick, his face softening, also nods hard for the pleasure of the Aged Parent. Over punch, Wemmick explains that he keeps his professional life at the office separate from his private life at Walworth, never mentioning one while involved with the other. At nine, the Aged P. gets his treat for the day; a cannon is fired by Wemmick and its resounding explosion shakes the castle. After an excellent supper, a night's rest, and some breakfast, Pip and Wemmick set off for Jaggers' office. During their walk, Pip observes that the closer they get to their destination, the harder and drier Wemmick becomes. By the time they arrive, the mechanical, post-office expression is so set on the clerk's face that Pip can hardly believe that the castle in Walworth exists.

COMMENT

It is worth noting here that, despite their difference in social status, Bentley Drummle rings a note not unlike that of Orlick. Both are sluggish, amphibious creatures, who keep to the dark. Pip's attitude toward the relatives of Miss Havisham reveals him to be conscious of the bad effects of desire for nobility and wealth in others (though not in himself). Wemmick proves to be a winning character, and at the same time, an example for Pip. In order to express the incompatibility of money, the law, and crime, with love and the imagination, Dickens gave Wemmick a life divided into two totally separate realms. In the office, where portable property and the interests of crime and law reign, Wemmick is a stiff, dry, mechanical little city clerk. His home, however, is removed from that and kept safe against the threat of the city by a dividing moat. The castle itself is a product of Wemmick's imagination, contrived to please the Aged Parent and to have a countrified air. Wemmick, like Joe, has worked with his hands to create this. In a sense, it seems that the real values of love and imagination are only possible among simple, virtually uncitified people such as Joe and Wemmick when at Walworth. Wemmick is even humble, like Joe, and cleans Pip's boots. While Pip does not yet consciously realize the basic truth that Wemmick illustrates, he certainly prefers the Wemmick at home to the dry city face of the same man.

CHAPTER 26

Pip is issued the invitation to dine with Jaggers. He is to bring his three companions to the office the next evening; then, they will go to Jaggers' house. When Pip, Herbert, Startop, and Drummle arrive, they find Jaggers scrubbing himself vigourously with scented soap. The lawyer always does this after dismissing a case or a client; as if to free himself from the dirt and infamy of his trade. Jaggers' house is stately and gloomy. Taking a close look at Pip's friends, Jaggers has an immediate interest in Drummle, whom he calls the Spider. He begins to talk to him. At this point, the housekeeper enters to serve dinner. Pip observes the tall, lithe, pale woman, with faded eyes and a mane of hair. She seems to be in her forties. Jaggers proceeds to preside over an excellent meal. Each time the housekeeper brings in a dish, Pip is struck by her strange expression of fierceness and fear and also by her manner of looking at Jaggers as if awaiting his orders hesitantly. While the dinner is a gay one, Jaggers soon manages to bring to the fore what is weakest in each of those present. Pip patronizes Herbert and boasts of his own prospects. By the end of the meal, Drummle becomes nearly ferocious in his sense of his own superiority and all are showing off their rowing arms. Suddenly, Jaggers grabs his housekeeper's arm. If they wish to see real strength, he says, let them all see Molly's hands. They are immensely powerful and one wrist shows evil scars. Molly is then dismissed. Jaggers singles out Drummle and drinks to him, with the result that the lawyer has the pleasure of seeing the morose man become more intolerable than ever. Drummle and Pip are soon involved in an ugly discussion of each other's spending habits. Jaggers ends the argument with the announcement that it is time for them all to depart. Pip returns, after the good-byes, to apologize to the lawyer. Jaggers replies that he likes the Spider and advises Pip to keep clear of him as much as possible. A month later, Drummle completes his studies and leaves the Pocket household.

COMMENT

The central topic of this chapter is the violence to be found in people. Molly, Jaggers' housekeeper, was clearly a proud and violent woman in her youth. Drummle, too, is arrogant and easily provoked to violence. Pip's guilty imagination grasps this element in both. Jaggers, forever conscious of a core of guilt in every man, uses this knowledge to uncover the weakness in each person present. It was probably through the use of this faculty of perceiving guilt that Jaggers tamed Molly. Guilt, violence, and pride are psychologically linked together.

CHAPTER 27

Pip receives a humble letter from Biddy, telling him that Joe is coming to London the next day. Biddy hopes Pip will see him. She adds Joe's message, "What Larks!" Pip does not think of the visit with pleasure. Rather, he feels mortified and would pay money to prevent it. His only relief is that Joe will only be seen by Herbert, whom Pip trusts, and not by arrogant Drummle. Pip has spent much money lately refurnishing his apartment. He has even obtained a servant, the son of a washerwoman whom Pip has decked out in livery, and whom he must now feed and try to keep busy. This servant boy, called the Avenger, is put on duty in the hall while Pip readies himself for Joe. Joe comes, his face aglow. Keeping a bewildered grip on his hat, he surveys Pip's rooms and is deeply impressed. His news of the town and their old friends is good except that Wopsle has left the church and joined the stage; he is now performing in London. Herbert soon arrives, and Joe is so disconcerned and confused that his wishes for Herbert's good health turn out garbled. Conversation over breakfast is very stiff. Joe begins to call Pip "sir," and jumps up frequently to replace his hat which keeps tumbling down from the mantle. By the time Herbert leaves for work, Pip is nearly out-of-temper with Joe. Alternating between calling Pip (affectionately) by his own name and, formally, "sir," Joe explains that he would never have come except to be of service and to deliver a message. Miss Havisham has asked Joe to tell Pip that Estella is home and willing to see him. As Biddy was unwilling to write this in a letter, Joe came in person. Pip blushes all the more because he would have been kinder to Joe had he known this were the reason for his visit. Joe now prepares to go. Dropping all formality, he apologizes to Pip for his behavior; explaining that they should only meet where it is private and things can be understood. Joe feels wrong in London clothes or anywhere except at his forge or on the marshes. With simple, undisguised dignity, Joe says good-bye. When Pip recovers himself, he goes to look for Joe in the street but cannot find him.

COMMENT

Pip's pride and property have begun to form the gentlemanly facade he so long desired. It is this facade that alienates Joe, making the blacksmith stiff and formal. Joe instinctively withdraws from pretensions that Pip had when a child, and not till they are alone, does Joe's old feeling for that child revive. His parting speech to Pip shows him to be far above any false values and makes Pip ashamed. But property has come to Pip and with it, pride. Having achieved this much worldliness, it seems that Estella's love may now be available. Attaining such love is the next step upward, and this is Pip's desire. Only when shamed into it does Pip remember the value of the love that Joe and evidently, Biddy too, still have for him. The themes of guilt and pride, and love and money are strongly restated; in both their true and innocent aspects as well as in their roles as parts of worldly experience and appearance.

CHAPTER 28

Pip decides to go back home, visit Estella, and stay at Joe's cottage. However, he soon begins a series of self-deceiving arguments. He persuades himself that to appear at Joe's so suddenly would be an imposition and that he needs to stay nearer to Satis House. Deceiving himself with these pretenses, Pip decides to stay at an inn called the Blue Boar and sets out for there. His companions on the coach are two convicts and Pip falters when he sees their familiar leg irons and gray dress. One convict has a half-closed eye and, with a start, Pip recognizes him as the man (with the file) who gave him money. The convict does not recognize him even though Pip's seat is directly in front of the man. After dozing off during the early part of the trip, he wakes and wonders whether he ought to give back the two pounds to this man. At the same time, he hears the convict discussing the very same incident with his companion. He learns, from their conversation, that the two pounds had been a gift from his convict of the marsh and not a mistake. Furthermore, his convict had asked this convict to deliver the money to the boy who had brought food and kept the secret. Filled with dread at this coincidence, Pip gets out as soon as the coach reaches his town. In his mind, he sees the slimy river dock for which he knows the convicts are headed. Pip heads for the Blue Boar. There, a waiter recognizes him and gives him a copy of the local newspaper. An article in it tells him that none other than Pumblechook is to be praised as Pip's patron and the founder of his fortune.

COMMENT

In his role of mature narrator, Pip begins the chapter by explaining his dishonesty to himself concerning Joe. By calling himself a swindler and a cheat, Pip's guilt is emphasized and he is placed on a level with criminals. Promptly, convicts enter the scene, and, once again, Pip is in close contact with the underworld. Memories of the scenes on the marshes come back to him. Pip no longer remembers his sympathy with his convict; only fear and a sense of degradation remain to accuse him. This is indicative of Pip's present state of mind. He had lost touch with such human sympathy as he had with his convict. He now sees the incident only from a snobbish social and moral point of view. He is criminally guilty, not because he associated with a criminal, but because his newly gained pride and sense of appearances let him deny a basic human bond to Joe. Thus, the theme of guilt and crime play a part in Pip's discovery of the two-pound gift.

CHAPTER 29

Pip is up early. Walking around Miss Havisham's side of town, he thinks that his patroness is adopting him, as she adopted Estella, and that she must intend for them to marry. He imagines himself a hero, marrying a princess, and restoring a castle. The core of his desires is Estella whom he loves because she is irresistible. He knows his love is beyond hope, reason, or even happiness. Pip rings at Miss Havisham's gate. To his total surprise, the door is opened by Orlick. The sullen man has left the forge to work for Miss Havisham and to live in a dark hole of a room on the premises. Pip proceeds down the dark corridor where he meets Sarah Pocket. She is still envious of him but only remarks that she hopes Matthew Pocket is getting wiser. Miss Havisham and her surroundings are unchanged, but an elegant lady sits near her. After a brief greeting, Pip realizes, in amazement, that the elegant lady is Estella. She is so much more beautiful and winning that Pip slips back again to feeling like a coarse, common boy and is overwhelmed by the distance between them. Greedily, Miss Havisham asks Pip if Estella has changed, reminding him that he had once wanted to go away because she was proud and insulting. The new Estella attracts him even more. Her pride has become a part of her beauty. Among the dreamy influences of a childhood now gone, Pip realizes that Estella is inseparable from his desires for money and gentility, his shame of home and Joe; therefore, she is inseparable from his innermost life. It is decided that Pip should spend the day there and he and Estella are dismissed to walk in the garden. Pip's feeling of youthful submission rankles in him as he observes Estella's air of superiority. When she cannot remember having made him cry, Pip cries inwardly again. Estella then tells him that she has no heart, no sentiment, no sympathy, or softness. As Pip protests, he sees in her alert, attentive face something that he has seen in someone before. He cannot place it, and when he looks again, the attitude is gone. Estella is insisting firmly that she is without tenderness and that he must believe this if they are to be thrown together from time to time. In the brewery, Estella points at something, and as Pip follows the gesture of her hand, the same dim suggestion startles him again and then passes. After a few turns in the garden, during which Pip is deliriously happy in the belief that this haunting, inaccessible girl is intended for him by his patroness, they return to Miss Havisham. Pip learns that Jaggers has come on business and will be back for supper. As if returning to the past, Pip once again pushes Miss Havisham's chair through the darkened rooms. The dinner hour approaches, and Estella departs to get ready. The moment she is gone, the old woman throws her yellowing arm around Pip's neck. Pulling his head down to her, she whispers over and over a vehement command to Pip. He must love Estella blindly, with utter submission and self-humiliation, even if it tears his heart to pieces. To Pip, the urgently repeated words, "Love her," sound more like hate, despair, and revenge. Miss Havisham loved this way and now, with a wild cry, she rises up, clawing at the air. Pip grasps her and seats her. The scent of soap fills the air and Pip turns to find Jaggers watching curiously. Miss Havisham, who is as awed by Jaggers as everybody else, composes herself. Pip explains his own presence and they go to dinner. Pip observes that, while Estella shows much interest (if some distrust) in Jaggers, the lawyer refuses to look at her directly and keeps much more to himself than usual. Later, over wine, Jagger continues to be silent, with an air of knowing something, an attitude that quite unsettles Pip. Sarah Pocket, overcome with envy of Pip's expectations, does not come to Miss Havisham's room. This leaves the two ladies, Pip, and Jaggers to play cards; throughout, Pip is distracted by the beauty of Estella, now fantastically decked out in Miss Havisham's jewels. At last, he takes his leave and is promised that he will be notified when Estella comes to London. All night, he hears Miss Havisham's words, "Love her," and adapts them to "I love her." He feels grateful to have been chosen for Estella, and his emotions are so rapturously high that he forgets how lowly he is behaving in staying away from Joe. Yesterday's tears for the blacksmith have been forgotten.

COMMENT

With foreboding persistence, Orlick appears in the center of Pip's life again. It is indeed the center for, in this chapter, Pip commits himself headlong to loving Estella. He realizes that the desires for money and gentility that have been a crucial part of his inner life stem from and focus on desire for Estella's love. As her name and the image of her carrying a lighted candle in the dark might indicate, Estella is Pip's guiding star in his expectations. It was she that instilled these desires and shames in him, and it is now she whom he desires. What Pip does not grasp consciously, it seems, is the hate and vengefulness in Miss Havisham's urging. If he recognized this, he would perhaps examine the values of such love. He might even reconsider his decision not to visit Joe on Estella's account.

CHAPTER 30

Over breakfast at the Blue Boar, Pip tells Jaggers all he knows of Orlick's character and recommends that Orlick be fired. To Pip's surprise, the lawyer prepares immediately to do so. As Pip wishes to avoid Pumblechook, he and Jaggers arrange that Pip will walk toward London and that Jaggers will stop the coach for him when they overtake him. Walking along the road through the village, various people stare at Pip in recognition. The worst of these is Trabb's boy who does not merely stare but also shouts out in pretended terror at Pip's dignity and prostrates himself in the dust as a mark of humility. As if this were not enough, Pip soon sees the boy rounding the corner and approaching him again, throwing himself at Pip's knees and evoking the laughter of all who see him. Again, Trabb's boy appears ahead of Pip on the street, this time strutting pompously in an ingenious imitation of Pip, and declaring affectedly as he passes, "Don't know yah!" So Pip departs; from his town, disgraced and embarrassed. He mounts the coach for London when it comes and sends a scathing letter to Mr. Trabb the next day. However, "his heart is gone," and when he gets to London, Pip sends Joe a penitential present of codfish and oysters. Back at the Inn with Herbert, Pip confesses that he adores Estella. This is no surprise to Herbert who has perceived as much since Pip came to London. However, Pip loves her more than ever now and has doubts, doubts raised not only by Estella's aloofness but also by the possibility that his benefactress may change her mind. Herbert comforts him by pointing out that Jaggers would certainly not be involved unless Pip's fortunes were a sure thing. Then, Herbert proposes something disagreeable—a suggestion that makes Pip feel the old marsh winds again. In view of Estella's nature and upbringing and the misery she can impart, Herbert advises Pip to forget her. Pip declares that this is impossible and changes the subject to Herbert's own situation. Herbert reveals that he is secretly engaged to a girl considerably below his mother's notions of family. Her name is Clara and she lives in London with her invalid father, a retired ship's purser with a healthy temper. Herbert wants very much to marry her, but he has no capital and no job. Pip resolves to help him as much as he can. Herbert promises to introduce Pip to Clara and both depart for the theater to see Mr. Wopsle as Hamlet.

COMMENT

Pip's newly affected facade is so completely and artfully laid bare by Trabb's boy that even the reader is delighted. By pretending first to be prostrated by Pip's dignity and then by imitating Pip's snobbishly aloof air, the boy strikes to the very core of his affectation and reduces Pip to nothing. Clearly, the boy is as perceptive of Pip's vain airs as Pip was in his youth of Mr. Pumblechook's. The result of the humiliation is that Pip strikes back meanly at the source of his embarrassment. He is, however, reminded of his guilt in not seeing Joe and even tries to make up for it. He deludes himself into thinking that a foolish gift will soothe the hurt he has inflicted on the blacksmith, and at least it does soothe Pip's guilty conscience. In sending the fish, Pip reveals his belief that such property can replace human values and responses. Still, we sympathize with Pip's feelings as he expresses them to Herbert.

CHAPTER 31

The performance of *Hamlet*, with Mr. Wopsle in the title role, is a dismal affair. Whenever the undecided Hamlet asks a question, the audience is ready with answers and with laughter. The loudest laugh comes at Hamlet's death, forcing Pip and Herbert to give up in their attempts to applaud. Both feel sorry for Wopsle, laugh in spite of themselves, and try to escape at the end of the performance. However, they are met at the exit by Mr. Wopsle's attendant who conducts them to him. Wopsle is now calling himself Waldengarver, and as his attendant helps him disrobe, he explains why he has requested their presence. He asks, in a tone nearly patronizing, how they feel about the performance. Pip replies, at Herbert's prompting, that Wopsle was "massive and concrete." Wopsle accepts this with dignity. He comments that audience reception should improve with time and that the loudest critic was paid for his blasphemies by a proud and envious actor in the company. Sympathetically, Pip and Herbert invite Wopsle to supper.

COMMENT

Wopsle, who feels he has great expectations in the theater, parallels Pip in becoming more pompous and patronizing than ever before. The audience reaction to his performance is one of ridicule—in the same way that Trabb's boy ridiculed Pip in the preceding chapter. Of course, Wopsle is a more exaggerated example of expectations and snobbism and is used by Dickens to emphasize Pip's folly. However, neither one learns anything by being laughed at, and Wopsle considers the audience in the same light that Pip considered Trabb's boy: ignorant of the higher things in life. Unfortunately, Pip is not in the habit of self-scrutiny, and while he sees clearly both the absurdity and the sadness of a man like Wopsle, he fails to draw any comparisons between his situation and the actor's. He is sympathetic (and behaves kindly to the man) because he fears ever being in a like position. Pip's own lack of certainty sometimes borders on the ridiculous, and this portrayal of Hamlet could be taken as a spoof of Pip's current state of mind. He has bad dreams about it and simultaneously about the unsuitability of Clara as a wife. He still does not perceive his own absurd snobbishness.

CHAPTER 32

Pip receives a letter from Estella saying that she will be arriving in London. Pip can scarcely eat until the day arrives; he is four hours early to meet the coach. While waiting, Pip meets Wemmick who is on his way to Newgate Prison. Pip decides to go with him. The prison presents an "ugly, disorderly, depressing scene," and Wemmick walks among the prisoners like a gardener among plants. His post-office face takes notice (while the men whisper to him) of whether they will be in full bloom for their trials. He tells Pip to take special notice of the man with whom he shakes hands. That person proves to be a portly army colonel who does not seem to be worried about his fate. Wemmick accepts an offer of a pair of pigeons from the man; they shake hands and say good-bye. Wemmick explains that the man was a counterfeiter and will be executed on Monday. He feels that the pigeons are a good piece of portable property. Wemmick explains further to Pip that part of Jaggers' power with these people lies in the fact that he keeps himself so high and distant, slipping a subordinate in to soften the blows with a touch of humor. They part and Pip returns to three more hours of vigil at the coach-office; during this time he wishes his guardian's abilities lay in another direction, and he wonders if he will always be surrounded by the taint of prison and crime. It seems strange that he has been, ever since the night on the marsh, touched by recurrences of that taint and that, even now, through Jaggers, it should permeate his fortune and advancement. He hates it and thinks hard about the contrast between the jail and Estella. He is still feeling contaminated by it when he sees her face and waving hand at the coach window. Again, there is a nameless, fleeting shadow of recognition in his first glimpse of her.

COMMENT

As Pip so clearly feels, crime and prison recur thematically. The specific crime here, and often elsewhere in the book, is coining, or forging a false article. Dickens uses this crime to emphasize Pip's crime of forging himself into gentility—a false attitude for him. Perhaps this is why Pip feels so strongly that he is tainted by crime for, aside from direct contact with it, he is guilty of a forgery in human appearance and values. He feels strongly that Estella is removed from such ugliness yet he, once again, recognizes something in her. Perhaps, although he does not know it, he recognizes a faint connection with something criminal.

CHAPTER 33

Estella seems still more beautiful and allows herself to be even more charming, than before. Pip is to take her to a part of London called Richmond. These are Miss Havisham's instructions, and they must be followed. In this, and is Estella's manner, Pip sees cause for even higher hopes. While resting over some tea, Estella tells Pip that she is going to live, at great expense, with a lady who will introduce her to society. Pip tells her that he is as happy as could be expected, without her, in his pursuits at the good Matthew Pocket's home. Estella reports that Miss Havisham's other relatives are not as free from pettiness as Matthew; they write incriminating letters about Pip to Miss Havisham. Their reports have no effect, and Estella laughs in pure delight at seeing the relatives thwarted. She has grown up with falsely sympathetic intriguers; they have sharpened her hate, but they can do nothing to mar Pip. She thanks him for keeping them busy in vain. On this, she gives him her hand, even lets him kiss her cheek; then, she becomes businesslike again. Soon, they set off for Richmond. Passing Newgate, Estella asks about it. Pip, who does not wish to admit to knowing much, says that Jaggers is in on Newgate's secrets. They agree that the lawyer is a dark and secret man. Estella is letting herself be attractive. She tells Pip that he has been mentioned to the lady with whom she is staying and that he is to visit her as he thinks proper. She is to report often to Miss Havisham on her progress and the effect of the jewels which are now hers. For the first time, she calls Pip by his name knowing well that he will treasure it. Estella is soon deposited at an elegant old house and Pip goes to the Pocket's home, his heartache growing worse.

COMMENT

Estella's business-like attitude, her greater charm, and remarks about the jewels reveal her as Miss Havisham's perfect instrument of revenge. She seems to fall in with Pip's idea that Miss Havisham is his benefactress, and she mocks the property-seeking relatives. Yet, to Pip, she is the light of love. Light has been, and is again, as with Joe's forge, the image of the good or desirable in Pip's eyes. He does not see how much Miss Havisham manipulates (but responds freely) to the attraction of Estella who is the center of all desire.

CHAPTER 34

Pip, in growing accustomed to his expectations, begins to take notice of their effect on others and on himself. Although he prefers to ignore it, his conscience bothers him about Joe and Biddy; he sometimes thinks that the old kitchen and forge fires suited him better to sit by than any since. Pip also notices that Herbert is beginning to be affected by his extravagances. They both begin to fall into debt. They join a club, called the Finches of the Groves, whose members seem to have no other purposes than to dine expensively and to quarrel with each other. Drummle is also a member. Herbert will accept no support from Pip and gradually, becomes quite despondent. The pair spend money for nothing and pretend to enjoy themselves although they rarely do. Herbert spends his days in the City but cannot find an "opening." In various attempts to face their affairs, Herbert and Pip begin to list their debts. Pip feels himself, at these times, to be a "first rate businessman: prompt, decisive, energetic." He makes it a practice always to exaggerate his debts so as to leave a margin. All too soon, however, both he and Herbert run through their margins and must make others, so the practice proves an expensive one. At the end of each session, Pip bundles up his and Herbert's bills and accounts. He tags them and puts them away with a feeling of accomplishment. In the serene lull after one such session, a letter arrives. It is from Trabb and it respectfully informs him that Mrs. Joe is dead and that his presence is requested at the funeral.

COMMENT

Again, Pip succeeds in being dishonest with himself, and this time, he involves the vulnerable Herbert in his dishonesty. For Pip is no better at business affairs than Herbert; rather, he has mastered the appearance of efficiency, and, as before, his facade deceives himself as well as others. Amidst such tricks with himself, it is no wonder that Pip sometimes feels again the attraction of an honest, simple life, as represented by the fires in Joe's forge and kitchen.

CHAPTER 35

The news of his sister's death affects Pip deeply, and he begins to sense her presence everywhere. It is not tenderness that he feels but a shock of regret, and with it, a deep need for revenge on her assailant. He writes Joe and goes home. Walking to the forge, Pip's memories of his sister are softened. The cottage, he finds, has been taken over by Trabb and Co., and the village people cluster around it to admire its somber appearance. Two men, dressed in black, guard the door and show Pip into the parlor where Mr. Trabb is busy draping hats in black. Joe, too, sits there in formal mourning and can murmur little beyond a reference to Mrs. Joe as a fine figure. Biddy is moving about quietly. Pumblechook, having stuffed himself with cake and sherry, shakes Pip's hand in a fawning way. While all are being lined up for the march to church, Joe whispers that he would have preferred to carry her to the church himself, quietly, but had been told that the neighbors would take it as a sign of lack of respect for the dead. Being commanded by Trabb to use their handkerchiefs, the procession behind the casket starts. The neighbors approve and nearly cheer. The attentions of Pumblechook and the excessive pride of the Hubbles at being in the procession prove annoying. At last, the churchyard near the marsh is reached, and Mrs. Joe is laid to rest. Pumblechook seems to think that Mrs. Joe would have been glad to have died had she known that a gentleman of fortune was to honor her funeral with his presence. It is not until the guests have left that the cottage feels wholesome to Pip. During a stiff supper in the parlor, Pip does his best to put Joe at ease. He feels that he has made a great concession when he asks to stay the night in his old room. Actually, Joe is pleased by the request. Walking in the garden with Biddy, Pip learns from the sweet girl the particulars of Mrs. Joe's quiet death. Her last three words were: "Joe," "Pardon," and "Pip." Biddy points out Orlick, and Pip is infuriated that Orlick is still pursuing her. Biddy tactfully reproaches Pip by saying that she had not written him of his sister's death because she thought he would not be interested. She cuts off Pip's offer of financial aid, and she praises Joe's uncomplaining, loving goodness. When Pip declares that he will visit Joe often now and asks that Biddy stop calling him "Mr.", the girl infuriates him, first by her silence and, next, by the slight disbelief in her echo of his words. In a "virtuously self-asserting manner," Pip demands to know what she means. He then professes to be shocked when Biddy reveals that she is not sure he will visit Joe. Pip is distant with her after this and during a wakeful night, he thinks of what an injury Biddy has done him. Taking his leave next morning, Pip sees the light in Joe's face and shakes his blackened hand warmly. The mists that rise as he walks tell Pip, however, that Biddy is right, and that he will not visit often. Indeed, he does not come back for a long while.

COMMENT

Dickens' portrayal of the funeral shows it as an accumulation of pomp and ceremony put on solely for the sake of the neighbors. It is a facade assumed to satisfy their desires for respectability. It is as silly as are any such appearances of dignity, notably Pip's. Again, Pip is aware of the vanity in the funeral but not in himself; nor does he censure his own impulses to servility or pride although he censures these same qualities in Pumblechook and the Hubbles. Pip's confidence in the powers of money is evident when he offers to help Biddy by giving her some. His confidence in his own good qualities also emerges. Pip is still deceiving himself and ignoring the folly into which property and pride have led him.

CHAPTER 36

Time goes on, Pip's debts mount, and before he knows where he is, he is twenty-one, and come of age. He is asked to visit Jaggers' office on his birthday and arrives there in an excited state. Jaggers congratulates him and then looks at him in a way that reminds Pip of his interview with the convict on the tombstone. Pip is not to be told who his benefactor is. Jaggers does point out that Pip is living expensively, is certainly in debt, and most probably does not even know how deeply in debt he is. Calling Wemmick in, Jaggers presents Pip with a bank note for five hundred pounds, which, Pip readily admits, is a handsome sum. Each year Pip will be given this amount, and no more, to live on. This is the arrangement until the coming of his benefactor which may be years from now. Jaggers again emphasizes his own role as a mere agent. The horrid plaster heads behind the lawyer's back seem to twitch as he tells Pip that he would be compromising himself if he were even to guess at when the disclosure will come. When it does, Jaggers will know without being told, and his role as agent will cease. Pip conjures up a lame explanation for Miss Havisham's behavior and ends the interview by asking the lawyer to dinner. Jaggers accepts and Pip goes to wait for him in Wemmick's office. He takes the opportunity to ask Wemmick for advice as to how he might help a friend get a beginning in commercial life. Wemmick's official advice is most discouraging, but Pip perceives a loophole. He asks Wemmick if his personal Walworth advice might differ. For that, Pip must visit Wemmick at Walworth, and before departing with Jaggers, Pip resolves to do so. Unlike his clerk, Jaggers takes office manners home with him, and dinner proves so unpleasant that even Herbert is left feeling melancholy and guilty when the guest has gone.

COMMENT

Although Pip learns little that is new upon coming of age, Jaggers' scrutiny makes him feel like a criminal, and the tone of the interview is not encouraging. This will later prove significant. Also, we are relieved to see, at last, some evidence of generosity in Pip. He has sorely neglected Joe, who brought him up and, in doing so has ironically behaved with the ingratitude Pumblechook predicted when Pip was only seven. Yet, Pip is going to try to help Herbert, and if it is a small gesture at this point, it does serve to regain our sympathy. The themes of expectations, property, and guilt pervade the chapter. Pip's chief expectation, to be informed of his benefactor's identity, is not met.

CHAPTER 37

On Sunday, Pip goes to Walworth and Wemmick's castle. The Aged greets Pip and expresses great admiration for his son's success at Law; their conversation proceeds with Pip nodding harder and harder. The converstation continues until Wemmick arrives with Miss Skiffins, a lady friend. This lady has a face to match Wemmick's in woodenness and a high regard for the Aged. Wemmick invites Pip to come see how the island looks in winter, and Pip takes this chance to ask his Walworth sentiments about helping Herbert. He tells the whole story of his association with Herbert, his good opinion of him, and Herbert's meager chances at any property. Pip adds that he would like to contribute a hundred pounds a year toward buying Herbert a partnership in a small firm. He asks Wemmick to use his experience and knowledge of men in lending Pip aid. Wemmick thinks highly of Pip for wishing to help a friend and promises to ask Miss Skiffins' brother, an accountant, to see what can be done. Pip and Wemmick return to the castle, where Miss Skiffins is preparing an enormous tea and the Aged is tending the toast. Warmed by the tea, everyone sits while the Aged reads aloud from the paper and is heartily nodded at. Throughout the reading, Wemmick's hand is forever stealing around Miss Skiffins' waist, being unwound by her, and replaced on the table. Pip soon departs. Hereafter, he sees Wemmick often with the result that Clarriker, a young merchant with a new firm, is found. He agrees to give Herbert a position and to accept secret payments from Pip until a partnership is bought. Herbert surprises Pip shortly with the news that a merchant named Clarriker is showing interest in hiring him. Pip's friend becomes happier each day until, at last, he takes the position and comes home so joyful that Pip cries secretly in happiness to see his expectations doing some good.

COMMENT

The visit to Walworth and Wemmick's double life again point up how Pip has divided his own life between the hardness of London and Joe's warm cottage. Unfortunately for Pip, and unlike Wemmick, he has chosen to favor the London facade rather than the honest rural life with its more real delights. Still, Pip's heart is for once in the right place, and he succeeds, at last, in doing some good with his property. This marks a new stage in Pip's growth and his attitude towards his expectations. He affirms Wemmick's life sincerely. He becomes capable of actions that are of no material benefit to himself, and he begins to value human beings more than property.

Gone is his faint jealousy of Herbert and his former secret pleasure at Herbert's less promising future. Pip grows.

CHAPTER 38

All this time, Pip's heart has been much occupied with his love for Estella. His spirit has visited the house where she lives even when he has not. Pip finds himself in the position of being familiar with, but not favored by, her. Estella uses him to tease her other lovers, and although they call each other by first names, Pip is often forced to receive only what attentions she might give a half-brother. He pursues her through endless parties and pleasures, and although he never has even an hour of happiness with her, Pip believes that being with her forever would be the ultimate joy. At times, Estella tells him with pity that he should take warning of her. Other times, however, she tells him that she must go to Satis House and that Miss Havisham wants Pip to keep her company on the journey. Such visits reveal Miss Havisham as more dreadfully fond of Estella than ever. She looks at the girl as if she would devour her. Miss Havisham, with the intensity of a sick mind, must hear and gloat over every man Estella has fascinated. Pip realizes fully now, and with a bitter sense of degradation, that Estella must take vengeance for Miss Havisham on as many men as possible; the girl will not be given to Pip until this is done. By this device even Pip, who will get the prize, is tormented. He now sees clearly the unhealthiness in that darkened house. Estella, however, endures Miss Havisham's fierce affection without returning it. When she withdraws herself from it, Miss Havisham breaks into infuriated ravings, accusing the girl of ingratitude and coldness. To this, Estella retorts with indifference that she is what Miss Havisham made her and that Miss Havisham must take all blame and praise. While the old lady shrieks accusations of pride and hardness at Estella, the girl can only reply with unyielding calm that she owes and gives everything she is to Miss Havisham, since she was not permitted to learn love, she cannot give love to her. In all fairness, Estella has never been false nor unmindful of her teachings. As Miss Havisham desperately tears her hair, Estella watches in wonder and proves her point rationally: she cannot understand or give an emotion when she has been taught that it will destroy her as it did her adopted mother. Pip leaves the room as Miss Havisham, a miserable ruin, sinks to the floor. When he returns, the two are reconciled. He spends the night at Satis House and is so haunted by Miss Havisham that he gets up in the night and leaves his room . . . only to come upon her. The ghostly figure of the woman carries a candle and enters the dining room where she paces unceasingly; moaning all the while. Pip passes the night with the sound of her steps and cries in his ears. From that time forward, while the argument is never revived, Pip observes that Miss Havisham begins to show a certain fear of Estella.

At a meeting of the Finches of the Grove, it becomes Bentley Drummle's turn to toast a lady. Pip is aghast when he hears the toast to Estella of Richmond; he accuses Drummle of not knowing her. It is decided that, if Drummle can prove he knows the lady, Pip must apologize. The next day, Drummle brings a note in Estella's hand, and Pip apologizes as he must. He is, however, pained to think that Estella would favor such a "sulky booby." He soon finds out that Drummle is paying close attention to her and that she plays with his affections as she does with others. However, the Spider lies in wait and occupies Estella's attention so well, at a certain ball, that Pip goes to speak to her about it. When he reproaches her, Estella only answers that it is not the fault of a candle when ugly moths and insects flock about it. Pip insists that she favors Drummle with looks and smiles such as she never gives to him. At this, Estella asks Pip angrily if he wishes to be ensnared and trapped like all the others; for it is only with him that she is honest. With this, Estella leaves and Pip's story continues with an event that has been coming ever since his childhood—long before he met either Estella or Miss Havisham. That event is now about to hit him like a ton of bricks.

COMMENT

Love for Estella remains the central force in Pip's life and, with it, the aspiration toward gentility. She continues to make him unhappy by not returning his love and by making him feel his lack of gentility. There is no joy for Pip in their continuing relationship; yet, she persists in ignoring Herbert's advice. It is pride, however, that dominates this chapter. Estella's pride is so deeply ingrained into her nature that she cannot love—not even Miss Havisham. Miss Havisham's wounded pride has been the cause of Estella's peculiar upbringing. For once, we see clearly that Estella has been raised as a weapon, invincible because she is free of the pains of loving. Now, we begin to understand the scheming of Miss Havisham's sick mind. Pride drives Pip to challenge Drummle, and it is Pip's pride, projected to Estella, that causes her toleration of Drummle in order to infuriate him. His aching heart aside, Pip seriously feels that Drummle is not worthy of her. Estella, as she herself observes, is a candle, and all kinds of insects are attracted to her light. The imagery continues; pride and love are intermingled in the light of that candle.

CHAPTER 39

Pip is now twenty-three and knows nothing more of the source of his expectations. He has ceased to study with Matthew Pocket, although he reads a good deal. He has no other occupation. Herbert is progressing, at Clarriker's, according to plan and is, at present, in France on business. They have moved out of Barnard's Inn into rooms at the Temple. It has been raining for a week. Pip settles down to read in the lonely rooms near the river with the weather at its worst. The wind sounds like blasts from a cannon; the lamps in the court and on the stairway are blown out by its force; and the red fires on the river barges are spread into splashes. When Pip hears footstep on the stair, he thinks it is his dead sister. Pip goes to the stairwell with his lamp. In answer to his call, a man's voice asks for Mr. Pip. In the dim light Pip sees a strange face, looking touched and pleased to see him. The man is a sea-voyager, about sixty, with iron-gray hair and a weathered face. He holds out his hands to Pip with gratified recognition. Bewildered, Pip lets him in and watches him glance around in a pleased manner. He hears his coarse, broken voice register disappointment at not being recognized. The man asks if anyone is near, and at this, Pip recognizes his visitor as his convict from the marshes. Pip wards off the convict's thanks, asks him to understand that their ways are now quite different, and offers him a drink before he goes. When, upon shaking hands, Pip gives the convict hot rum and water, he is amazed to see tears in the man's eyes. He feels reproached, apologizes to the convict for speaking harshly, and wishes him well. They clasp hands. Pip learns that his convict has made a fortune on a sheep ranch in Australia. The man then asks him how he has come to do so well since the time on the marsh. Now, Pip's voice trembles as he explains that he has been given property, but that he does not know who has given it to him. His heart beats wildly and he jumps from his chair as he hears the convict name Pip's yearly income since he came of age, name Jaggers as the appointed guardian, and say that he got Pip's address from Wemmick. When he hears that the convict is his benefactor, Pip faints. As the convict helps him, Pip hears the grating voice explain tenderly that, when a hunted dog, the convict had vowed to help Pip and that he has now made the boy rich and a gentleman. Pip feels only dread at the news. Yet, the man goes on, naming himself as Pip's second father and describing his life as a shepherd and how he kept seeing, in visions, the boy who brought him food. He exults at having seen to it that Pip can live like a lord. Pip is relieved that the old convict is triumphant enough not to notice Pip's own reactions. The man admires Pip's ring, his linen, his clothes, and the fine books he reads. When he draws his sleeve across his eyes and his throat clicks in the way Pip remembers, Pip's blood runs cold. He asks Pip if he loves a lady, and Pip thinks in silent agony of Estella. The convict then assures him that, if money can't buy love, such a fine gentleman can surely win it. In Australia, the convict prospered slowly; in his mind, he triumphed over the insults of the better-bred colonials by remembering that he owned a London gentleman while he bolstered his heart with the knowledge that he would, one day, visit and make himself known to his gentleman. The convict has risked his life to be here now, and he and Pip must be cautious to prevent his discovery—for discovery means hanging. This is the last straw for Pip who now realizes that he is bound to protect the life of this man he abhors. As he goes about, preparing Herbert's bed and closing the shutters against peering eyes, Pip almost expects his convict to start filing at a leg-iron. Once the convict is in bed, Pip stares stunned into the fire until he finally realizes how wrecked his life is. Miss Havisham's intentions were a dream and Estella is not intended for him. He has been used to sting greedy relatives and as a practice-piece for a girl's charms. His deepest pain, however, is that, for the sake of a low convict, he deserted Joe. Although he now needs the comfort of Joe and Biddy, he is so conscious of his own worthless conduct to them that he could never ask for comfort. It now seems to Pip that, for weeks past, he has been seeing this convict's face in every crowd. He remembers the convict's desperation on the marsh and is in terror for his own safety, alone with a criminal. Gradually, Pip slips to the floor in an exhausted stupor and then wakes, still wretched. The candles and the fire have gone out and all is darkness.

COMMENT

The black wind and rainy night form a setting that is appropriately reminiscent of Pip's childhood meetings with his convict on the marshes. Dickens has carefully recreated the imagery of cannons and torches to prepare for the convict's entrance. Pip's imagination, also, is vividly alive as it was in his childhood. The candles and the fire, images always of Estella and of Joe and his forge, are symbolically extinguished at the end of the chapter, leaving Pip in darkness. For the discovery of his benefactor's identity shuts off, for Pip, any possibility of attaining the heights of gentility and love as they are epitomized by Estella. It also excludes all hope of returning to Joe's serene, honest, rural life. These two things that have been Pip's inner life, his desire and his guilt, are wiped away by blackness and by the the source of his fortunes. Pip sees that by helping the convict he began the long path of guilt and deception that he has followed since. This has led him to the point where he deceives himself and is so guilty of pride that he no longer recognizes his guilt. The convict has made Pip what he is and Pip, who had disliked bondage to Joe, is now in bondage to a criminal and responsible for the man's life besides. In the previous chapter, we saw that Miss Havisham made Estella what she is out of pride, to make right the wrongs she had suffered, and to allow herself to live, through Estella's actions, the life she desired. Pip's convict has done exactly the same thing to Pip. By the power of the money that accomplished the transformation from boy into gentleman, Pip became a piece of property, owned by the convict. Similarly, Estella is owned by Miss Havisham. However, neither Pip nor Estella is able to love his or her owner. The very pride and desire for money and love which have held sway over Pip have their roles in the emotional make-up of his convict. They have prompted him to make and own a gentlemen and so to participate vicariously in the life he never lived. The vices now recoil on Pip, punish him, and possess him quite literally in the person of the convict, rather than Pip's possessing them himself.

STAGE THREE

Pip's first waking thoughts are full of the pressing need to keep his dreaded visitor safe. He realizes that he would only arouse suspicion by trying to keep the visitor concealed so Pip resolves to pass the convict off as his uncle from the country. This decided, Pip goes down to the watchman's lodge for a lantern and, in descending the staircase, stumbles over a man crouching in the corner. The man remains silent and eludes Pip in the darkness; causing him to run to the watchman. When they return, the stairway is empty. Pip takes a light and searches his chambers. However, he finds no one and nothing is disturbed. His questions to the watchman, though, reveal that Pip's "uncle" had been accompanied by another person; a man in dust-colored clothes and a dark cloak. Pip pretends to take this news lightly. The next morning, Pip learns in whispers that the convict's real name is Abel Magwitch but that he is going by the name of Provis. He had no one with him when he came but he did notice that someone entered the gate alongside him. As the convict devours his breakfast uncouthly, Pip is again reminded of an old dog and he loses his own appetite. The meal finished, Provis again grasps Pip's hands; saying that his only stipulation for having made Pip a gentleman is to be allowed to stand by and look at him. Pip begins to see more clearly the aging man he is "chained to." Throwing a wallet full of money on the table, Provis declares that his only pleasure will be to watch Pip spend it like a gentleman. This is something the convict, himself, has never been able to do. In a frenzy, Pip stops this flow of talk and asks Provis what is to be done about protecting him from recognition and danger. Provis apologizes humbly for his low talk of money. He assures Pip that there are few people who would recognize him on the street. If the danger had been fifty times as great, Provis would have come anyway. As to how long he plans to stay, he has come for good. He will use disguises, if necessary. To be found out is death:

he knows it well and hopes Pip understands it. However, he has dared much in life and is too old to be afraid to dare death. Pip decides that, when Herbert returns, he will find a room nearby for the convict. Herbert will have to be told (and Pip secretly hopes for some relief in the telling), but Provis cannot consent to this until he has met the fellow and taken his oath on the black Testament he carries. After some discussion as to how Provis should be dressed, the guise of a prosperous farmer is settled upon. Next, Pip goes out. He rents a floor for his uncle in a nearby house with windows facing his own. He buys the clothes necessary for Provis' disguise and lastly, he visits Jaggers. Pip asks for verification of what he has been told—that Abel Magwitch of New South Wales is his benefactor. With downcast eyes, he pleads to know why he has been led to believe that his fortune came from Miss Havisham. To this, Jaggers mentions that there was no evidence of it and that Pip ought to take nothing on appearances. He tells Pip a little of his dealing with Magwitch and ascertains, in his cagey manner, that a man called Provis has delivered the news to Pip. Pip and his guardian say good-bye and Jaggers looks very hard at Pip as he leaves. Pip returns to find Provis enjoying his common habits of drink and tobacco. The clothes arrive and, the more Pip dresses Provis, the more his fugitive-slouch seems to emerge. Pip even notices that he drags one foot (as if it were chained) and that every mannerism of the man is that of a prisoner. The fonder Provis grows of Pip, the more revulsion Pip feels for the man who made him. At last, one night Pip hears Herbert coming. He restrains the convict who has jumped up with his knife drawn. Herbert comes in like a breath of fresh air to Pip but stops in wonder at the sight of the visitor; who is pulling out a Testament and asking him to swear secrecy. Herbert does so at Pip's bidding, and he and Provis shake hands.

COMMENT

There is much in this novel that paints a picture of the perfect gentleman for us. The Finches of the Grove furnishes a fine example of the type of frivolity that is characteristic of the type. Pip has not actually become such a gentleman though his convict thinks he has. Provis, on the other hand, is the epitome of all that is ungentlemanly. He is worse than coarse and common; he is a convict. If nothing else, Pip has attained a gentleman's snobbishness, and he is repulsed. The repulsion is increased by Pip's sense of being owned by and indebted to this man. He reacts to Provis' disguises as he did to Joe's Sunday dress, but he does not, as he did at one time with Joe, recognize the dignity that is hidden by the new clothes. He sees only that the furtive character, which is best hidden, shows through. Yet, there is much in Provis (and the reaction he causes) that cannot help remind us of Pip's first interview with that certain lady whom he had believed for so long was his benefactress. They both frighten Pip deeply, and perhaps this is because both are motivated by kinds of revenge. Certainly, both present an extraordinary appearance, and appearances have always affected Pip. This very aspect is brought out by Jaggers. The lawyer has adhered to the letter, if not the spirit, of his agreement. Pip's disappointment is his own fault for he has allowed himself to be deceived by appearances. His own faith in appearance has caused his pride and his guilty treatment of Joe. Now, it is the cause of part of the misery that confronts him. The crime and punishment theme with which Pip has been so involved has begun to relate directly to him.

CHAPTER 41

As Pip tells the secret of his expectations, he sees his own astonishment and repugnance mirrored upon his friend's face. When the tale is told, Provis' evident pride in having made a gentleman serves only to widen the gap between himself and the two young men. Provis, however, is sure that they are as proud as he. Again, he apologizes for being "low" about money and promises to keep a muzzle on himself. When, at last, Pip walks him to his lodgings and sees him safely in, this becomes his first moment of relief in days. Herbert sympathizes with Pip and both recognize in the other an unspoken aversion to Provis. They begin to consider what to do. Pip is heavily in debt and is fit for no calling, but he cannot bear to take any more money from his benefactor. Both feel that Provis is determined and desperate and that, if Pip were to disappoint him, Provis would turn himself in to be hanged and leave Pip to suffer as his benefactor's murderer. Even if Provis were caught by chance or error, Pip would feel wretched with guilt. The only thing to be done is to get Provis out of England. Pip must wait and break with him after he is gone. After breakfast the next morning, Pip asks Provis about himself and also about the man he fought in the marsh. As he prepares to tell the story, the convict reminds Herbert of his oath and comments that his own crimes are paid for.

COMMENT

In "muzzling" himself, Provis is doing his best to suit his ways to the life of two gentlemen, and to hide the magnificently fierce Magwitch. Indeed, we will see very little of that larger-than-life part of the man from now on, and he will seem less and less the convict of the marshes. Pip, however, is now in a position similar to that of his childhood. Once again, he fears the forces of law and must make an effort to help a criminal. Once again, he is involved in guilt, and, this time, he is threatened with being guilty of a kind of murder; caused by his own negligence. Negligence has been Pip's crime against Joe, but in this case, the more serious consequences make Pip unable to disappoint Provis. Pip's entire life and ambition, since the coming of his expectations, is revealed in its true light. The light shows them to have been based, not only on self-deception, but also on disreputable foundations. No true gentleman can emerge from crime.

CHAPTER 42

This is Provis' story. His entire life has been a series of jailings, whippings and cartings to and fro. He does not remember any parents or home; rather, his first memory is of stealing turnips for food. Everyone who saw him was frightened by his appearance, and after being jailed a number of times when he stole to avoid starving, he became known as "hardened." He grew to manhood doing many things, none of which paid and all of which led to trouble. He became acquainted with a man named Compeyson who was educated, bred as a gentleman, and handsome—the man whom he hates and with whom he was fighting in the ditch. Compeyson took him as a partner in his business. The business was swindling, forging, or anything the gentleman could do and blame on someone else.

With Compeyson was a dying man named Arthur. The two had once made a great deal of money out of a rich lady, but they had gambled most of it away. Magwitch was soon much involved in Compeyson's dealings by doing what Compeyson planned. He was always in danger and always in debt to the man. Even Magwitch's wife objected. Once, he went to jail for doing Compeyson's dirty work while Compeyson went free. Later, they were both arrested on the same charge. At the trial, Compeyson looked and behaved like a gentleman while it was clear that Magwitch was only a common wretch. All the evidence pointed to Magwitch, and the differences in their appearances and backgrounds were stressed. The verdict for Magwitch was guilty while mercy was recommended for the gentleman. His sentence was half the length of Magwitch's. Then and there, Magwitch vowed to get his companion in crime. They were on the same prison-ship, carefully separated, but the only time Magwitch got near Compeyson, he scarred the gentleman's face. Shortly afterwards, Magwitch escaped, and the incidents on the marsh took place. Magwitch saw to it that they both went back, but at the trial, he was given a life term and, again, the gentleman got off lightly. Magwitch has never heard of him since. As the emotional man gathers himself back into being Provis, Herbert passes Pip a note. It says that Arthur was Miss Havisham's brother and Compeyson the man who professed to love her.

COMMENT

Provis' story knits the plot together and commands our attention because of the new information it brings out. The tale also reveals much about the convict. He, like Estella and Pip, was an orphan, an outcast from society. However, Provis had no one to care for him. Utter poverty and lack of love drove him early to a life of crime, as it might have done to Pip had there been no Joe or Mrs. Joe. The incident of Compeyson's gaining mercy from the law did more than arouse Magwitch's hate; it instilled in him a very basic and cynical grasp of the advantages of being brought up a gentleman. In the official world and the courts, appearances and manners are all-important. They can even be a matter of one's lifelong freedom. So, to make Pip a gentleman was the greatest kindness, the greatest advantage that the convict could find to bestow. Facade counts for character in the eyes of the world. It took a child to be kind and responsive to a beaten man of harsh exterior, and, in Pip's innocence, he was better able to see beyond facades than he is now with his experience in the world. For this innocence Provis is so eternally grateful that he is unaware that Pip's natural response to him has disappeared with his innocence; it was, in fact, removed by the gift of expectations.

CHAPTER 43

Much of Pip's shrinking from Provis is caused by the abyss he now feels between himself, who harbors a convict, and the proud beauty Estella. Pip resolves never to mention her to Provis and turns his mind to the problem of Compeyson. That man, as Pip knows, must live in deadly terror of Provis. If Compeyson knew his enemy had returned, fear (if nothing else) would prompt him to inform the law. However, before Pip can act, he feels he must see Estella and Miss Havisham. He pretends that he must go to visit Joe and sets off on a misty day for Satis House. The first person Pip sees at the Blue Boar is Drummle. They both pretend not to see each other, and Pip is bitterly sure that Drummle has been visiting Estella. Pip decides to confront Drummle. They are conscious, all the while, of trying to shoulder each other out of the warmth of the Blue Boar's fire. Drummle reveals, with insolent triumph, that he is to dine with Estella. He also suggests that Pip keep his temper as he has lost enough already. Pip forces himself to keep silent, and soon both men are forced to give their places at the fire to incoming guests. Drummle leaves and mounts his horse, and Pip notices that his attendant wears dust-colored clothes. The attendant's build, posture, and gait remind Pip of Orlick. Feeling out of sorts, Pip washes and sets out for Miss Havisham's.

COMMENT

Pip shows himself capable of using Joe as a false excuse. He is extremely jealous of Drummle, and not without reason, for Drummle is clearly having some success in courting Estella. A foreboding mist envelops all the action of the chapter.

CHAPTER 44

Pip finds Miss Havisham and Estella seated in the dressing room and, from the glance the women exchange, he perceives that they see some change in him. Pip says that he has come to speak to Estella and that Miss Havisham shall hear it, in a moment. He is now as unhappy as Miss Havisham could have intended. He knows his benefactor, and the discovery has made him miserable; nor will it enrich him as it still remains a secret from all others. From Miss Havisham, Pip learns that Jaggers' role as his benefactor's lawyer as well as her own was mere coincidence. She allowed Pip to believe her to be his patron because it suited her purposes to punish her relatives in this manner. Miss Havisham points out that Pip made his own snares. Pip proceeds to tell this ancient lady that she wrongs the Pockets, Herbert and Matthew, who are all generous and incapable of mean designs. He is gratified to see her look up keenly and ask what he wants for the Pockets. Pip then asks her for money to complete the purchase of Herbert's partnership but without Herbert's knowledge. After a long silence, Miss Havisham asks, "What else?" Pip turns to Estella's immobile face and declares his great love for her. He can do this now without any hope. Had Miss Havisham known what pain, hope, and torture she was causing, he would accuse her of hideous cruelty. He believes, though, that the lady's own trials made her forget his. Estella answers that his words of love do not touch her heart as she has warned him. She does not love Drummle, either, but she is going to marry him. Pip struggles to control his feelings and, in looking up, he is impressed by the ghastly expression on Miss Havisham's face. Earnestly, Pip pleads that, Estella at least, should marry someone who loves her. Estella looks at him in wonder and asks if she should fling herself on a man who would soon suffer at the total lack of response in her. Once more, Pip tells Estella that she is part of his life, part of every dream and yearning, and that her influence is so deep that it forms the good and evil in his character. The words gush out in an ecstasy of pain; he takes her hand and he leaves. Yet, he never forgets the wonder in Estella's face, nor the pity and remorse in Miss Havisham's. Feeling that all is done and gone, Pip walks the entire way to London. He arrives at the Temple after midnight. The night-porter has a message for him. The deliverer has requested that he read it before going to his rooms. The note is in Wemmick's handwriting and reads simply: "Don't go home."

COMMENT

This chapter ends Pip's hopes for Estella's love but not his agonies. During their conversation, she calls him a "visionary boy" and, indeed, Estella has been the force in Pip's visions. Miss Havisham's pity and remorse are genuine, and we realize that Pip is right about her. She is not deliberately cruel; rather, she is so involved in her own sorrow that she has forgotten the feelings of others. She has even made Estella unfeeling to the point where she is as incapable of joy as she is of pain. Wemmick's warning note ends the sorrowful chapter appropriately, as all does seem done and gone.

CHAPTER 45

Pip turns away immediately and finds himself a room in a poor section of London. In bed and exhausted, in "the gloom and death of the night," Pip cannot sleep. He hears creaking noises from every piece of furniture and, before his eyes, loom the words "Don't go home." He believes he is sleeping in the bed of a recent suicide and he looks for blood. However, despite Estella and their parting, Pip's mind can only wonder and consider the command not to go home. He rises early and heads for Walworth. Wemmick is having a cheery breakfast with the Aged. In a round-about way he tells that, while at Newgate, he heard rumors that Magwitch had left Australia; that Pip's rooms had been watched and would be watched again. By whom, Wemmick cannot say, but he feels sure that any such watching concerns Magwitch. In giving information, Wemmick is restrained by a certain loyalty to his office, so Pip makes clear that the clerk may refuse to answer (as he sees fit) the questions Pip will ask. Wemmick answers them with nods; letting Pip know that Compeyson is alive and in London. Upon having heard the rumor, Wemmick went to Herbert and advised that he hide Provis in another part of the city until Pip returned. Herbert proposed to take Provis to Clara's house where there was an upper floor for rent. The house is out of the way, and Herbert can bring Pip news of Provis without exciting suspicion. As the house is on the river, it provides an easy means of escape to a foreign boat (when the time comes). Herbert made himself busy and by nine o'clock, the visitor had been housed at Clara's. Word had also been left at his old lodgings that Pip's uncle had been summoned to Dover. Thus, anyone following Pip's movements would have been miles away on a wild goose chase. Suspicion was thus diverted and confusion was increased by Pip's not going home. Wemmick gives Pip the address of the place where Provis hides; saying that it will be quite safe for Pip to visit him this first night. When he's there, Wemmick advises Pip to get a hold of the portable property. Wemmick leaves for work, and Pip spends his day dozing with the Aged by the fire. He leaves after supper and many nods.

COMMENT

Much has been done to forward the plot, and the chapter is full of Dickens' favorite devices. Pip's nightmarish night with its obsession over the note is a good example; so is the Walworth humor of Wemmick and the Aged. Yet, even at Walworth, Wemmick is in favor of obtaining portable property whenever possible. The problem of identity and names is played up in Wemmick's insistence upon referring to Provis as "Tom, Jack, or Richard." It brings up the question of who Provis is and who Magwitch is, for they seem quite different people. It even implies a question as to which one is Pip's benefactor. Provis, Pip, and Estella are orphans, and while we know Pip's parents, we can only guess at Provis' and Estella's. Pip, like Wemmick, has to deal with dual persons within himself. Questionable identity pervades this chapter and the novel as a whole.

CHAPTER 46

By eight o'clock, the pleasant scents of a dock tell Pip he is near his destination at Mill Pond Bank. After losing himself several times among old ship hulks, he sees the tall wooden house with bay windows. His knock is answered by a pleasant landlady, but Herbert soon appears. He takes Pip to the parlor, shuts the door, and tells him all is well. An alarming growl and the scent of rum from overhead, indicate the presence of Clara's father, who, despite his gout, persists in weighing out all food provisions as he used to do on shipboard. His name is Mr. Barley, but Herbert calls him Gruffandgrim; he is Clara's only relative. Only Mrs. Whimple, the kindly landlady, knows of their affection. As they converse, a captivating dark-eyed fairy of a girl enters, and Herbert blushingly introduces Clara.

In Clara's basket, neatly parceled out, is her supper and her father's breakfast for tomorrow. Pip finds, in Clara, a winning modesty. He is most pleased at Herbert's engagement to her, but, as he gazes admiringly, Clara runs off, called by the stamp of a wooden leg on the ceiling. Herbert now accompanies Pip upstairs where Provis is comfortably settled. Provis is not alarmed and seems, to Pip, to have softened indefinably. Pip does not tell him that Compeyson is in town, but he relays all the rest of Wemmick's news and advice. Provis answers everything calmly and swears, by anything that comes from Jaggers' office, to keep hidden and to see Pip rarely. Pip promises to come with him (or to follow soon after him) when he escapes abroad, and Provis concedes that this is no time for Pip to begin greater expenditures. Herbert then has an idea. As he and Pip both row well, they could easily take Provis down the river when the time comes. Pip decides to keep a boat at the Temple and make it his habit to row on the river. Provis is never to recognize him if Pip comes down to Mill Pond Bank but to signify all's well by pulling his window shade down.

With that, Pip and Provis say gentle good-nights, and Pip is surprised that his own heart is heavy and anxious at their parting. He takes leave of sweet Clara and the motherly Mrs. Whimple, and as he retraces his steps, Pip is struck by the redeeming youth and hope in the house. He thinks sadly of Estella. The rooms at the Temple show no evidence of watchers, and Herbert's report, when he comes in, confirms this. Next day, Pip gets a boat and begins to row daily regardless of the weather. The first time he passes the wooden house, the shade comes down promptly. Herbert's reports give no cause for alarm, but Pip continues to feel watched and to fear for the rash old man down the river.

COMMENT

Clara, like so many of the characters in this novel, has no family to speak of. Old Barley lives in the past and hardly behaves like a father. Clara and Mrs. Whimple are in clear and exact contrast to Estella and Miss Havisham. The problems of identity and place (in both society and the scale of human values) are raised by the comparison. Clearly, simple goodness, warmth and honesty are not compatible with property and pride. Pip's own identity is unfolding. Not only is he taken with Clara and Mrs. Whimple, he finds much feeling in his heart for Provis as well. Pip has regained some of his childlike human sympathy and responses. Provis no longer represents a degrading threat to Pip's chances for love. Pip can now respond to him on human rather than social terms and he finds that he feels much for the aging man who has tried so hard to be good to him.

CHAPTER 47

Weeks pass. Nothing changes and no signs come from Wemmick. Pip's creditors begin to press him, but Pip is still unsure in his mind and cannot accept more money from his patron. With wavering inconsistency, Pip avoids all newspapers that might assure him of Estella's marriage although he feels sure that it has taken place. Pip's dread of Provis' discovery continues to be unsupported, and, to relieve his restlessness and suspense, he rows often. One evening, having seen the all's well sign in Provis' window, Pip docks his boat and resolves to visit the waterside theater where Mr. Wopsle is causing the drama to decline. Wopsle, who plays an admiral, a miner of thunderbolts, and an Enchanter, sees Pip in the audience. Pip observes, with surprise, that, whenever Wopsle has no stage business to attend to, he stares with amazement in Pip's direction. The glare of mounting confusion that Pip sees in the actor's eyes serves only to confuse him. He is still wondering about it when, upon leaving the theater, he finds Wopsle waiting for him. In greeting him, Mr. Wopsle promptly asks Pip who else was with him. This alarms Pip, and he presses for details. Wopsle was sure that Pip was with the man who sat like a ghost behind him until he observed that Pip was unaware of the presence of anyone. Pip, who has every reason to be chilled by Wopsle's words, resolves to be silent while Wopsle makes himself plain. Wopsle however, is sure he won't be believed. Hesitantly, the actor describes the chase through the marshes, the fighting convicts, and the torch-light of that day long ago. Pip admits to remembering it all well. The face Wopsle saw, behind Pip in the theater, was the face of one of the convicts. Steadying himself, Pip asks Wopsle which of the two and Wopsle replies readily that it was the younger one; the one who had been torn in the face. Summoning his own acting powers, Pip declares that the sighting is curious, but not alarming. Pip treats the actor to a drink and they part. No one is near Pip as he enters the Temple. He tells Herbert about it and they write Wemmick a letter telling of the incident. Both Pip and Herbert become more cautious than ever.

COMMENT

As in his childhood, Pip is once again the victim of numerous terrors. The ghostly appearance of Compeyson behind him seems vaguely like one of Pip's childhood nightmares come to life. The heightened, almost super-reality of the incident recalls the vividness of Pip's imagination and impressions when he was young. However, there is nothing imaginary about this threat.

CHAPTER 48

A week later, after docking his boat again, and after looking about him for a place to eat supper, Pip is overtaken by Jaggers.

The lawyer asks Pip to join him for a meal and Pip decides to do so on hearing that Wemmick is coming, too. At Jaggers' house, Pip tries to catch Wemmick's eye but finds it impossible. A note for Pip from Miss Havisham has come; in it she asks him to come to visit her about the business matter he mentioned. Wemmick mentions that, if Pip goes at once, he needn't write. Taking this lead, Pip decides to go the next day. Jaggers brings up the matter of the Spider having won Estella and observes that, of the pair, the stronger will win. If Drummle relies on his intellect, he will lose, but if he beats his wife, he will win; for a fellow like the Spider either beats or cringes. His words cause Molly, the housekeeper, to become very upset. Pip is struck by Molly's resemblance to Estella. He becomes absolutely certain that Molly is Estella's mother. Jaggers notes Pip's painful reactions. The housekeeper comes in twice more, briefly, and Pip's conviction becomes more certain. The evening is a dull one, and Wemmick is all post-office in manner. Together they leave early, and after a few steps, the Walworth Wemmick replaces the other. Pip inquires about the Aged and Miss Skiffins. Pip next asks Wemmick about Molly. He is told that twenty years ago, Molly was tried for murder and acquitted, thanks to Jaggers. The case made him the success he is. Immediately after her acquittal, the woman entered Jaggers' service, as tamed as she is now. A child, allegedly belonging to Molly, had been a girl and was not seen again. Wemmick has no news concerning Provis except that he got Pip's letter. They say good night and Pip goes home to ponder.

COMMENT

Pip's fancies are still running high and he fears for Provis. This can be seen in his vision of hanged clients at Jaggers' office. The discovery of Estella's birth and mother is significant. Pip can hardly help but be affected by the news that this proud girl comes from worse parents that his own. Not only were her beginnings coarse and common—they were criminal.

CHAPTER 49

As decided, Pip goes to Satis House on the following day. He finds Miss Havisham with her ragged chair pulled close to the fire into which she stares. She seems utterly lonely and Pip feels pity for her. At last, she glances up, sees Pip, and asks, "Is it real?" When he assures her, she thanks him, and he sees a new expression on her face. She wants to prove to Pip that she is not all stone. Pip reassures her and Miss Havisham asks him to explain what useful and good thing he would like her to do for his friend. Pip tells her of the secretly bought partnership for Herbert and how he is now unable to make the final payments. Miss Havisham asks how much money he wants and promises to give him nine hundred pounds for the purpose if he will tell no one of her part in it. When Miss Havisham asks if he is unhappy, Pip's voice fails. He manages to say that part of his unhappiness comes from other secret business. Miss Havisham gives him a note ordering Jaggers to pay Pip the money, a note that makes it clear that Pip is not profiting by the transaction. With trembling hands, she gives him her gold pencil also, hoping that he can write under her name the words, "I forgive her." She prays him to do so, even if she is long dead. Pip exclaims that he can do it now. To Pip's terror, the ancient woman drops to her knees at his feet in an attitude of prayer. He begs her to rise, but she only clings to his hand and weeps in despair, "What have I done!" Pip cannot comfort her. He also knows well what evil her diseased mind has done. However, he can only feel compassion for this woman who has punished herself in the vanity of her sorrow. The ruined Miss Havisham gasps out that she saw, in his face, what she once felt herself. When the cries die away, Pip pleads that she try to restore Estella to her true self. Pip asks how Estella came to her. In a cautious whisper, she says that Jaggers brought the two-year-old orphan when she told him that she wanted a little girl to love. Pip is convinced now of the identity of Estella's mother. Miss Havisham's mind is eased and there is a new and affectionate tone of compassion in her voice. They part and Pip goes to stroll in the garden. In the decaying brewery, Pip sees again, with a shock, the vision of Miss Havisham's body hanging from a beam. The vision prompts him to go back up and see if Miss Havisham is well. She is sitting by the fire, but as Pip withdraws to go, a great flame shoots up and envelopes Miss Havisham in flames. She runs toward him, shrieking and enveloped in fire. Pip tries to save her and succeeds in putting out the fire. Pip holds her until the surgeon comes. She is pronounced badly wounded but more endangered by nervous shock. She lies on the table where she proposed to lie dead; her burnt bridal garments exchanged for cotton wool. She seems a phantom and repeats endlessly: "What have I done," "I meant to save her from misery," and "Write under my name 'I forgive her.'" At six in the morning, Pip kisses her just as she murmurs the last of the phrases. Pip leaves for London.

COMMENT

When first begun, Miss Havisham's mourning was a kind of pride. She reveled in inflicting sorrow and suffering upon herself. However, the atmosphere she made worked so on her mind that the vanity became an evil vengeance. She has committed great wrongs with both Estella and Pip and her newly gained consciousness of this causes such abject suffering that Pip can only forgive. He, too, is guilty of a pride and self-involvement that took no consideration of the pain of others. His realization of this is a difficult step to take. The fire that consumes Miss Havisham comes as a culmination of all the images of fire in the book. Having deeply and painfully repented, the fire becomes the flames of her redemption. She is left without pride—with only the mere spirit of her old vanities. Furthermore, her mind can only punish itself repeatedly with the consciousness of the evil she has inflicted. Pip, too, has suffered burns for his own pride which he recognizes and condemns.

CHAPTER 50

Pip has burned his left arm badly while saving Miss Havisham and must carry it in a sling. Herbert tends Pip with a kind devotion for which Pip is grateful. It is Pip's memory, full of impressions of the fire, which pains him the most. Pip is also worried at the thought of not being able to row the boat. Herbert tells Pip that Provis is improving, growing more gentle and communicative. He has told Herbert about the dark, wild part of his life, spent with a young, jealous, and terribly revengeful woman who was tried for the murder of a stronger woman found strangled in a barn. Jaggers defended her and she was acquitted. She and Provis had a child whom Provis loved deeply. On the night of the murder, the woman came to Provis, swore to kill the child, and vanished. (Pip is breathing hard at this point.) Provis tells Herbert that he is sure that she did just that; but that he loved and pitied her anyway. This woman disappeared after the trial and so Provis lost both mother and child. Pip, excited to a fever pitch, now tells Herbert that Provis is Estella's father.

COMMENT

Pip has put considerable effort into uncovering Estella's parentage. Ironically, his own patron, the convict Pip had shrunk from earlier, is Estella's father. Her birth matters much to Pip. Only by being sure that it was an ignoble one, will he be able to rid his mind of the seeds she planted there—seeds of guilt, shame, pride, and aspiration to money and gentility that have since replaced the solid human values in Pip's life. The problem of Estella's identity is, in this way, crucial to the basic themes of the novel.

CHAPTER 51

Pip wants to go to Jaggers and get the complete truth about Estella's parentage. However, he cannot say if he wants it for Estella's sake or to lend romantic interest to the convict he is trying to save. Early in the morning after his conversation with Herbert, Pip heads for Jaggers' office where he finds the lawyer and Wemmick working together. It is first necessary that Pip recount the disaster at Miss Havisham's and to show the order that nine hundred pounds be given him. Jaggers signs the check and says he is sorry Pip is not to have any money for himself. Pip tells the lawyer that he asked Miss Havisham not to give him any. Both Wemmick and Jaggers disapprove. For the first time, Pip now has the lead in conversing with Jaggers. He tells the lawyer that he knows Estella's mother and he knows Estella's father, too. This brings Jaggers to an attentive halt for even he does not know her father. The man's name is Provis, and he is from New South Wales. Jaggers starts but represses his surprise and asks Pip on what evidence Provis bases his claim. None, says Pip, for he doesn't know his daughter exists. Jaggers glares sternly at Pip who explains how he has pieced the story together, only omitting Wemmick's role. He appeals to Jaggers to be frank. Pip's life has been concerned with Estella for so long that whatever concerns her affects him. When Jaggers remains immovable, Pip turns to Wemmick, asking for Wemmick's help in persuading Jaggers to be more open. Jaggers sighs and admits the truth, swearing both Wemmick and Pip to secrecy. Pip and Wemmick both promise secrecy. The clerk and the lawyer resume work with odd glances at each other; both more rigorously professional than ever. Both are relieved when a client, Mike, comes in with news that his daughter has been arrested for shoplifting. The men move on to new business.

COMMENT

The problem of Estella's identity is now solved to Pip's satisfaction, and, for once, he has had his way over Jaggers. It is only necessary that Pip know the secret so as to bolster up the changes that are taking place within him. He has no need to reveal the secret. Jaggers, who knows so many mysteries and who cannot speak directly, reveals himself clearly in the case he puts to Pip. Like Wemmick and Pip, too, Jaggers has a divided life. Hidden, within, are the very human feelings that Pip has so long been dead to and which he is just beginning to trust again. All are guilty of varying degrees of hypocrisy. It is the hypocrisy of denying emotion that allows the lawyer and his clerk to maintain their professional manners. Property, they both agree, must be coveted if only to protect one's interests. Here, Pip takes the major step of disagreeing. Pip's attitude to property has come to be much like Joe's. It has little value and cannot be compared with the human value of Miss Havisham's testimony to him. Estella is no longer a daughter of the gods to Pip; the desire for property and gentility he learned from her has dimmed. These themes fade, and are replaced by the virtues for which Joe has always stood.

CHAPTER 52

Pip now goes directly to conclude his dealings with Clarriker. He now has the satisfaction of seeing completed the only good he has attempted since the arrival of his expectations. As partner in the firm, Herbert will be sent to establish a branch in the East. Pip must prepare to separate from his friend. Herbert comes home, full of joy and the news of his good fortune. Pip's burns heal, but slowly. One Monday at breakfast a note comes from Wemmick suggesting that Wednesday might be the day to try to help Provis escape. They will ask Startop to replace Pip at the oar. Pip thinks he will go with Provis, and, as destination does not matter, they will take the first steamer they can. He and Herbert familiarize themselves with the vessels leaving by Wednesday's tide. Pip gets passports, and Startop agrees to help row while Pip steers. Herbert will go to Provis the night before and instruct him to come down to the water when he sees them Wednesday. However, returning to his rooms, Pip finds an anonymous letter. It dares him to visit the sluice-house in the marshes alone if he wants information about Provis. Pip scarcely considers. He must take the coach in half an hour or else lose his chance completely.

For all he knows, not to go would bring harm to Provis. He just has time to check on Miss Havisham (who is a little better) and to eat dinner at the town inn before setting out for the marsh.

COMMENT

By helping Herbert, Pip has accomplished the single good action of his expectations. In deciding to go with Provis, he has made up his mind to stand by an essentially good man despite appearances or old crimes. His decision is strengthened when he finds that he must risk a trip to the marshes just on the chance of helping that endangered convict. Pip now recognizes that a man like Pumblechook is a master of false good appearances and a man like Joe is a good man who has no facade. Clearly, Pip is discerning that appearances are as worthless as property. He again affirms the human value.

CHAPTER 53

It is a dark, windy night and the marshes seem so dismal that even Pip is oppressed. He is half inclined to go back. He hurries toward the abandoned, run-down sluice-house, noticing the ghostly way in which the choking vapors from a nearby kiln creep toward him. Pip knocks, waits, and knocks again, but there is no answer. He tries the latch and the door opens, but no one answers his call within. Suddenly, the next thing Pip knows, he is caught in a strong noose, thrown over his neck from behind. A voice then says, "I've got you." Arms pull his arms close to his sides. This causes Pip's bad arm to pain terribly. Struggling and crying out in the dark, Pip is bound tight to the ladder that leads to a loft above. He is faint and sick with pain. His captor lights a candle. It is Orlick. With a deadly look, Orlick calls Pip his "enemy" and says that he means to "do it" by himself. Orlick accuses Pip of having had him fired from Miss Havisham's and of coming between him and Biddy by giving him a bad name with her. Pip fears for his life as it seems that Orlick means to kill him and burn his body in the nearby kiln. Pip looks wildly for a way to escape but there is none. He thinks of the consequences of an anonymous death —Provis will curse Pip for deserting him, Herbert will doubt him, and Joe and Biddy will never know how sorry he is for having turned away from them. Orlick confesses to Pip that it was he who attacked Mrs. Joe because he was envious of how Pip was treated. Pip sees that Orlick is drinking himself into a murderous state, and he continues to make confessions to Pip. He revels that it was he whom Pip stumbled over on the stairs the night of Provis' arrival and that he has fallen in with Compeyson, who wishes Provis dead. With a sudden motion, Orlick throws away the bottle and picks up a heavy stone hammer. Pip shouts with all his might and then struggles with renewed violent force. In the same instant, he hears responsive shouts, sees a light, and a group of figures. When he comes to from his blow, he sees the face of Trabb's boy. Herbert is supporting his head and with him is Startop. They rebandage Pip's arm and help him back over the marsh to town. Orlick has fled. Pip learns that, in his hurry, he had dropped the note from Orlick in his room at the Temple. Herbert and Startop found it soon after. Both were so alarmed that they hired a small carriage and followed. There was no news of him at Miss Havisham's but Trabb's boy was found and agreed to guide them to the sluice-house. They had feared to enter at first, but when they heard Pip's shouts, they lost no time. Preferring not to be detained for any reason, all three make light of the matter to Trabb's boy and pay him well. They do not stop to see to Orlick's arrest but take the same small carriage back to London. Only Pip's anxiety about Wednesday's plans prevents his complete collapse. He spends Tuesday in bed; feverish, nervous, and in great pain. Exhausted, he sleeps well and wakes feeling strong and healthy as Wednesday dawns.

COMMENT

Once again, ghosts and visions visit Pip's imagination, and he is afflicted with fear; as he was so often in child-

hood. Clearly, the fear is well founded. The genuine-
ness of Pip's change is evident here, for, as death
approaches, his thoughts are for Joe, Biddy, Herbert,
and Provis. He regrets bitterly that he will not have time
to clear away old guilts and to set things back on a true
course based on his new and human values. Orlick
blames Pip for his own crimes and, though the accusations seem hardly credible, they are worth considering,
for, indirectly, by being better loved and respected, Pip
has shaped Orlick's life much as Provis shaped Pip's
and Miss Havisham shaped Estella's. Orlick wishes to
kill the Pip with the expectations, but Pip, like Miss
Havisham, emerges from near death with his new views
firmly fixed in his mind. Still, Orlick is not absolved
from guilt for the fellow is undeniably criminal no matter how or by whom he was driven to be so. Nor is Pip
absolved from the crime of his pride; he will suffer much
to pay for it.

CHAPTER 54

Pip sets off for he knows not where. He has a few necessary
things packed in a bag, and his mind is wholly fixed on Provis'
safety. The plan is to row down the river, stay overnight some-
where, and catch one of two steamers leaving London with
the outgoing tide Thursday. Pip feels hopeful as their boat
moves briskly along. Passing the steamers they might hail
tomorrow, they soon come to Mill Pond Bank. The shade is
pulled down, and they only need touch shore, for Provis is
waiting. He boards and they push off. Provis puts his arm
thankfully around the faithful Pip. They make their way past
busy docks and crowded waters, Pip carefully watching for
any sign of suspicion or followers. There is none and they
reach clear waters evidently undiscovered. Provis refuses to
trouble himself about danger until he meets it, and he looks
forward to seeing Pip the best gentleman in any country to
which they go. He is now happy just to be free and with his
boy, and Pip realizes how much it took for the old man to risk

freedom for any reason. Just at Gravesend, in marsh country like Pip's, they put ashore for a short rest and some food. The journey continues until nightfall, and Pip searches the flat, lifeless horizon for a lonely tavern at which to spend the night. Herbert and Startop, both exhausted, continue to row slowly. They are now below the point where ships are searched and any place will serve to hail the steamers. In the gathering darkness, the entire company is sure they are being followed. They start at each splash of the tide. At last, they see the light of a dirty, solitary public-house. Over dinner by the kitchen fire, the landlord asks if they saw a four-oared galley (a large rowboat) pass them going upstream. It had two men sitting in it. Although they wore no badges, the Jack is sure they were Custom House officers. This news makes Pip very uneasy, especially since the galley must still be hovering about. After seeing Provis to bed, he decides, with Herbert and Startop, to stay at this inn until the first steamer is due, when they will put the boat out into the steamer's path and drift with the tide till it comes. Waking in the night, Pip glances out of the window and sees two men looking at their boat. Worried, he watches them until they disappear back across the marshes. At breakfast, he tells his companions of this. Provis seems unconcerned about the Custom House men, but he and Pip decide to walk to a point of land and have Herbert and Startop pick them up there in the boat. As they walk, they talk little, but the convict's manner is relaxed and it is Pip who watches for the mysterious four-oared galley. Herbert and Startop pick them up and the smoke of the two steamer's soon becomes visible. As Pip shakes hands in farewell to Herbert and Startop, a four-oared galley shoots out from a bank and moves into the steamer's path ahead of them. As the steamer approaches, the galley hails them and a voice cries that in Pip's boat is a man named Magwitch (wrapped in a cloak) whom they wish to arrest. Meanwhile, the steamer, almost on top of them, stops its motor but comes on with the tide. In that instant, Provis stands up and pulls a cloak away from the hidden face of one of the people in the galley. It is Compeyson who is white with terror. As the two enemies tilt backward, there is a warning from the steamer and Pip's boat sinks under its prow. In an instant, Pip is pulled aboard the galley along with Herbert and Startop. Finally, Magwitch, who is severely injured, is recovered, pulled aboard, and handcuffed. Compeyson is not recovered from the water. The officer who ordered the arrest takes charge of all the convict's belongings including the pocket-book. Pip alone is allowed to accompany the prisoner to London, and Pip feels sure that his place is at Magwitch's side as long as the man lives. His repugnance has melted away. The hunted, wounded, shackled prisoner is his benefactor. Pip sees him now as affectionate, grateful, generous, constant through the years: in all, a far better man than Pip has been to Joe. As he watches Magwitch groan and struggle for breath, Pip half hopes the man will die of his wound. If not, he will be hung for certain. Pip vows never to leave Magwitch's side unless forced to and to be as true to the convict as the convict has been to him. The old man trembles to hear this, and Pip makes a private vow never to tell Magwitch of the loss of the money.

COMMENT

The marsh-country setting harkens back appropriately to the first scene of the book when Pip met his convict. Even then, Pip feared the young convict, whom he now knows was Compeyson, more than he did Magwitch. Magwitch is much softened since that time, but the old raging violence returns at the sight of his enemy. He becomes his former self long enough to fulfill his vow of hate and kill him. The problem of Magwitch's identity is solved here. Once the object of his hate is dead, the violence within him dies forever. He becomes his best self. Taken prisoner, he is once more a convict as when Pip first knew him; yet, at the same time, he is Pip's benefactor. Pip fully acknowledges and accepts him as benefactor now. However, the money is gone and, with it, the last dreams of any property and gentility that have so long plagued Pip and made him a lesser man than he was capable of being. Ironically, that loss is a gift. At the same time, Magwitch has helped Pip learn the very qualities he failed to learn from Joe and to respect these as true dignity. All Pip's reverence for appearances is gone, and he is able to give himself to a man who appears ignoble. In a sense, the gallows that haunted Pip's dream as a child, and repulsed him at Newgate as a youth, have also become a reality. They threaten Magwitch's life and, as such, threaten Pip's happiness. The criminal is no longer a matter of shame and guilt; for Pip recognizes his own crimes. The themes of property, gentility, shame, guilt, pride, and dignity (both true and false) are resolving in Pip's mind.

CHAPTER 55

Pip hires Jaggers for the convict's defense. The lawyer is angry with Pip for having allowed the money to slip away. While he will not tell Magwitch, he insists that an attempt be made later to reclaim it. Pip resolves not to sicken his heart by trying to claim the money. When Compeyson's hideously disfigured body is found, in his pockets are found notes concerning Magwitch's large bank account and valuable lands in Australia. Clearly, he had hoped to collect these. Magwitch is committed with his trial due in one month. At this dark time, Herbert comes with news that he must now go to Cairo to set up a branch office. He must go soon; he cannot even wait for Clara's father to die and their marriage to take place. He must come back for her afterward. This departure is no surprise to Pip, and he assures his anxious friend that he will be spending much time with Magwitch and, so, will be less lonely. Herbert raises the question of Pip's future (which now leads nowhere) and delicately offers the position of clerk at the Cairo branch. He wants Pip to come with him; even Clara has begged that Pip come. Pip, however, cannot think clearly now and has a vague idea of his own about his future. He asks Herbert to wait three months for his answer; Herbert gladly assents. That same week, Pip sadly sees Herbert off. As he returns to his empty rooms, he meets Wemmick who has been knocking at his door. Wemmick bemoans the loss of the portable property, and Pip bemoans the loss of its owner. They share a drink and Wemmick, in a fidgety way, tells Pip that he is taking his first holiday in twelve years on Monday. He almost begs Pip to take a walk with him then—between eight and twelve in the morning of that day. Despite his desire to be alone, Pip accepts. He arrives at the castle to find the Aged out of bed and away and Wemmick looking tighter and sleeker than usual. They walk and, suddenly, Wemmick seems surprised to see a church. Upon convincing Pip to enter the church, they find the Aged and Miss Skiffins inside. An idea seems to dawn on Wemmick and he says, "Let's have a wedding." A clergyman appears and, struck by a notion, Wemmick finds a ring in his pocket. The ceremony proceeds; broken only by the Aged who is giving the bride away and does not hear his cue. There is a good breakfast afterward at a pleasant tavern, and Pip sees that the new Mrs. Wemmick no longer unwinds Wemmick's arm from around her waist. Pip wishes the bride and groom well and departs after assuring the groom that he will not mention this Walworth sentiment at the office.

COMMENT

Jaggers' role toward Pip and his convict-patron has come full circle now. Wemmick's wedding is a delightful interlude. It and Herbert's departure serve to make Pip's being alone emphatic for the two were his London friends. Property, too, is definitely and finally dispensed with. Pip has no more desire to be contaminated and pained by worldly goods. He is left with human sentiments and a life without expectations.

CHAPTER 56

Magwitch lies, very ill and in pain, at prison where he awaits trial. As it hurts him to speak, he speaks little. Pip visits each day so he notices the wasting and weakening of the man whom he loves. Magwitch never justifies his life to Pip; he wonders only, if under better circumstances, he would have been a better man. His smile shows that he trusts in Pip's seeing some redeeming qualities in him. At the trial, Pip holds the convict's hand. The trial is short and clear and Magwitch is found guilty. At the day of sentencing, Magwitch is a major attraction for he will get the death sentence. Thirty-two others will be sentenced, too. The Judge gives a long and special address; denouncing Magwitch's case and condemning him to die. A shaft of sunlight falls in the court. It reminds Pip that everyone present, the Judge included, must face with equality the absolute Judgment. Magwitch stands and says, "My Lord, I have received my sentence of Death from the Almighty, but I bow to yours." Pip cannot rest until he sends petitions to all the men of authority who might be able to help Magwitch's case. He prays that the prisoner will die before his hanging. He visits Magwitch daily. The prisoner lies placidly with no light in his eyes. He answers Pip by squeezing his hand. On the tenth day, his eyes light up to see Pip, and he speaks clearly, blessing his boy for never deserting him. Pip is silent, remembering how he once meant to desert. What's best, Magwitch thinks, is that he has felt more comfortable with Pip in these dark times than he did when all was well. Pip tells Magwitch the child he loved and lost is alive—a beautiful lady now whom Pip loves. With a last effort, Magwitch raises his hand to Pip's lips. It drops to his side again and his head drops quietly to his breast. Pip can find no better parting words than, "O Lord, be merciful to him a sinner."

COMMENT

Magwitch has true dignity in death. He has taught Pip so much humanity that Pip really does give of himself— a new and good experience for him. He has become capable of much love and humility—to the point where the lie with which he eases his benefactor's death transcends the truth. It is a return to the innocence of the novel's beginnings but the innocence is enriched by maturing experience.

CHAPTER 57

Pip is now wholly alone and seriously in debt; he determines to leave his expensive rooms at the Temple and sell the furnishings. To make things worse, he is ill. After a night of delirious terrors and visions, the vapors of the kiln, which had once threatened to consume Pip's dead body, begin to clear from his mind and he sees two strange men staring down at him. They have come to arrest him for debt, but Pip cannot get up to go with them. He sinks into fever again. Many people visit him and against some he struggles, believing they are murderers. All of them look vaguely like Joe. As the illness passes its worst point, Pip's delusions change and vary but all people who tend him persist in looking like Joe. At last, he has the courage to ask, "Is it Joe?" And the dear old voice answers that it is. At this, Pip's heart breaks and he begs Joe to be hard with him for his ingratitude. However, joy is all Joe feels, and he only says, "Ever friends," and, "What larks!" Pip whispers over and over, "God bless this gentle Christian man." Gradually, he learns he has been sick almost two months and that Joe has tended him during most of it. Pip learns that Miss Havisham has died. She left her property to Estella; except four thousand pounds for Matthew Pocket. This was because of what Pip had told her of Pocket. The legacies to the toady relatives did not exceed twenty-five pounds and were all jokes. Orlick broke into Pumblechook's house, took that gentleman's money, drank his wine, slapped his face pulled his nose, and committed various other indignities, all leading to Orlick's arrest and imprisonment. Joe talks to Pip now with the simplicity, confidence, and unasserting protectiveness that Pip recalls from childhood. They both look forward to the day when Pip can take a ride—as they once looked forward to the day of apprenticeship. When the day comes, Joe carries Pip out like a child. The beauty of June and the Sunday bells make Pip more thankful than ever to the blacksmith. As Pip becomes stronger and better, however, Joe becomes less at ease with him. The fault is Pip's, for he has long taught Joe's innocent heart that when Pip is strong, Joe has no hold on him and had better loosen and let go before Pip himself withdraws. Though Pip sticks fast to his old manner, Joe is soon calling him "Sir." Pip dares not tell Joe of his financial straits, for, even if it removed the tension, Joe would insist on helping him from his own meager savings. Pip and Joe spend an evening pondering and making separate resolutions. Pip decides to tell him all the very next day about his hopes for a certain marriage and his plans for helping himself as Herbert's clerk. However, Joe leaves before he can tell him of his plans so Pip must follow Joe back to his town. Once there, Pip plans to apologize humbly to Biddy to ask her to marry him.

COMMENT

In the coma of his sickness, Pip's past cruelties plague him terribly, and he suffers his guilt many times over. Even his identity, which has undergone so many changes, now seems uncertain and mechanical. It is a suffering Pip must endure before becoming wholly transformed from a gentleman of expectations to a man of feeling. Joe nurses him as Pip nursed Magwitch, and the final reproach to Pip is Joe's departure. The reasons are evident, and Pip must humble himself still more before the real sickness (that of his spirit) can heal. All vestiges of pride must disappear. The penitence that plagued Pip's youth must visit him again. Many loose ends are tied up as Joe brings Pip up-to-date. Both Pumblechook and Orlick get their due, and, remembering Pip's own feelings about Pumblechook, we feel that Orlick's last action was his most justifiable one. All is laid in readiness for the final scenes.

CHAPTER 58

News that Pip's fortune has fallen has reached his home town. At the Blue Boar, Pip notices the explicit cooling in demeanor toward him. He is still weak and the trip has exhausted him, but the best bedroom, always saved for him, is not available this time. Before breakfast in the morning, Pip strolls to Satis

House and discovers that everything there is being put up for auction. Pumblechook awaits Pip at breakfast. He shakes Pip's hand with magnificent forgiveness saying he is sorry Pip is brought low. He adds that he expected nothing else. He has the air of a benefactor resolved to be true to the last and annoys Pip with his attentions; finally, Pip asks the fishy gentleman to leave him alone. This causes Pumblechook to bewail loudly (to the edification of waiter and landlord) this wretched, prodigal boy for whom he cared so much as a child. As Pip has come to the final indignity of going to Joe, Pumblechook advises Pip loudly to tell Joe that today he has seen the founder of his fortunes. It is someone who bears no malice to the ignorant Joe or the ungrateful Pip. His earliest benefactor sees, in Pip's being brought low, the reward ingratitude deserves; yet, he is glad at having been benevolent. At this point, Pip observes acidly that he has not seen his benefactor at all today. He then leaves the imposter to rant to his audience. The incident serves to brighten still more the forbearance of Joe and Biddy. As Pip approaches the cottage he feels, with relief, that he has left arrogance and untruthfulness behind. His heart has softened, and the countryside fills him with peace. He hopes to see Biddy at the schoolhouse before she sees him. However, school is closed for a holiday. Listening for the clink of Joe's hammer, Pip is surprised that the forge, too, is still and closed, He is fearful but, seeing the best parlor window open and decked with flowers, he looks in. Joe and Biddy stand there; arm in arm. Biddy cries out as if she sees a ghost, but soon she and Pip embrace with tears. Pip remarks how well she and Joe look and how smartly dressed they are. Both beam at him, and Biddy bursts out in joy that today is her wedding day; she is married to Joe. Shock makes Pip's strength fail. Touched, proud, and overjoyed to see him, the pair help him to a seat and apologize for having surprised him so. His coming makes their day complete, and Pip is silently thankful for never having mentioned his hope to Joe. Pip tells them that he will go abroad and work for money to repay his debt, but nothing can cancel his real indebtedness.

When they have children to love, Pip hopes they will not think of the first little boy in that house as unjust; rather they will know that the grown boy honors them both. Pip means all he says. His touching words melt the hearts of Biddy and Joe, and they forgive him. Later, in London, Pip sells all he has and goes to join Herbert as a clerk. His first responsibility is sole charge of the firm while Herbert leaves to marry Clara and bring her back. Pip lives happily and frugally and is constant, always, to Biddy and Joe. When Pip is made third partner in the firm, Clarriker insists on telling Herbert the old secret. The news is happily received. Pip realizes that the ineptitude he had seen in Herbert's business sense was his own fault, not his friend's. They are all comfortable and prosper without getting rich.

COMMENT

As the man with the most hypocritical facade in the book, Pumblechook shows his true colors. Pip sees well the "impostor's" lack of value as a human being and recognizes his own past folly in respecting appearances. It is worth noting that Pumblechook had nothing to do with the convict having given Pip property; instead, he merely introduced Pip to Satis House and thus began Pip's miserable delusions. Pip's reaction to the marriage of Joe and Biddy, his genuine joy and lack of jealousy, give final proof of the transformation in his heart. He, like Magwitch, has softened into humanity. This, and his humility, show him to have done his penance thoroughly and to have redeemed himself. He sets about to make his own modest life rather than having a life made for him. In doing so, Pip finds the happiness he has missed since the beginning of his expectations.

CHAPTER 59

After eleven years, Pip returns to Joe's cottage. He looks in at Joe and Biddy and a happy scene. Joe is as strong as ever. Sitting beside him, on Pip's fireside stool, is a child who seems to be the boy Pip himself once was. When Pip joins them after a warm greeting, he learns that the boy is, in fact, named Pip. He and his namesake take a walk in the morning and understand each other perfectly. Pip wishes the boy were his, but, when he and Biddy talk of marriage, Pip tells her he sees no hope for it. He says, in answer to Biddy's question, that all his poor dreams of Estella are gone although he has heard that Drummle is dead. Pip visits Satis House. The old grounds are in twilight, but Pip can see the places where house, garden, and brewery had been. Coming along the garden path is a solitary figure. Pip draws nearer, hears his name called, and sees Estella! Her fresh beauty is gone, but the majestic charm remains and the light in her proud eyes has softened. They talk softly, and Pip remembers his last words to Magwitch and the dying man's expression. Estella tells him that these grounds are her last possession and that she has come to see them one last time before builders change them. In taking leave of the place, she had thought also to take leave in her heart from Pip. He has been in her heart while suffering has bent and broken her into a better shape. However, she had a great lesson to learn from what Pip's heart used to be when, in the pain of loving her, he still forgave her. Pip takes Estella's hand in his, and, as they walk in the mist, he can imagine "no shadow of another parting from her."

COMMENT

Pip's desire for Estella and the life she stood for are gone; only genuine feeling remains. She, like Pip, has softened; suffering has given her a heart with which to love. She and Pip will now be able to share their lives in a way that was at one time impossible for either of them, especially together. As they leave the ruins of the old house, they leave the ruins of their former selves. The mists, which rose when Pip began the new life of his expectations, now rise again, as if in recognition of the beginning of yet another new life.

CHARACTER ANALYSES

PIP

An understanding of Pip is essential to an understanding of *Great Expectations*. He is, at the same time, the central character (the changes in whom are the central subject of the book) and the narrator, through whose eyes we view the actions and events of the tale. His position as both central character and narrator is a curious one. It brings us into close contact with him immediately and from more than one angle. We have, simultaneously, the adventures, thoughts, and feelings of the boy and young man and the more mature reflections of the Pip who is actually relating the story. This union of the two voices in one enables us to enter into the complexities of Pip's character from the very opening lines. These lines give us the information that he is an orphan and, as such, is a character living outside the normal lines of home and family. We are soon introduced to the two chief influences on the child: Joe Gargery and his wife, Pip's sister. The examples they set for young Pip take strong hold in his character as is seen clearly later in the book. Joe gives him a sense of honesty, industry, and friendliness, along with generosity and dignity. Mrs. Joe, with her concern for property and pomp, contributes more than is ever mentioned to his desires and ambitions. Pip's general personality as a child is clear. He is depicted as good-natured, intelligent, and extremely imaginative and thoughtful. With the entrance into his life of outside influences (at his first visit to Miss Havisham's) he becomes discontented, ashamed of what he is, and ambitious to change. The effect of these feelings is immediate in his view of those around him. The false values, which he is pressed into accepting by his desire for Estella and his shame of being common, begin to eat away at his regard for Joe. These ideas fester within him until he learns of his great expectations. What follows can be simply expressed; he goes to London and becomes a snob. There are, however, some redeeming factors, such as his frequent guilty moments when he thinks of Joe and Biddy, but he is always able to fool himself into ignoring them with some excuse. He is still, however, able to discriminate in his choice of friends and gains some who help him in his various hours of need. He meets Wemmick in London but cannot take this man's example of how to live in a society of criminals. His alienation from Joe (and the true values Joe represents) builds through Stage Two of the novel. He becomes selfish, greedy, foolish, and a spendthrift. The process he goes through in making out his bills illustrates his ability, at this point in his career, to fool himself successfully, and to turn his face away from reality toward what is basically empty and false. His helping Herbert Pocket secretly to a position is the only good thing he accomplished with his wealth.

When Magwitch is revealed as the source of his expectations, a new phase begins in Pip's life. Pip is revolted by the man and can feel no longer the human sympathy for him he once felt naturally on the marshes. He has changed and can only think of himself, of his degraded position and his destroyed hopes. However, it is through the tie he has with Magwitch, and the life he spends with him from that man's arrival until his death, that Pip learns again many things he had forgotten and some new things as well. Magwitch is his true benefactor, not in money but through the devotion and love he and Pip come to share. After his death, Jaggers' suggestions about somehow getting hold of his property sound hollow in Pip's ears. His concern had come to be with the man and not with any expectations that the man could provide. Through Magwitch, he learns the full truth of Estella's parentage as well, and through this knowledge, comes to know that his aspirations were falsely based.

Magwitch's property is forfeit to the crown and Pip is to be arrested for debt. However, he is too ill to go to prison. At this almost hopeless point, Joe arrives and, through his selflessness and devotion at Pip's bedside, becomes the second great teacher Pip encounters. Joe tends him and leaves before being thanked. This reinforces for Pip all the values he had as a child sensed in Joe but could not fully understand. We know of Pip's life after his recovery that he becomes a clerk and eventually, a partner in Herbert's firm. He has suffered much and grown in understanding of himself and others. For this reason, he is now able to reap the fruit of his one good act performed while he was wealthy, after first having reaped in full the evil seeds he had sown. Pip's marriage to Estella is also only possible because of the change in him, his development into a man who can love for natural rather than selfish desires, who can give as well as receive. Domestic life such as that of Biddy and Joe becomes possible for him as does honest labor. He, too, like Joe, is a working man. He has discovered (or rediscovered) the ultimate value of human relationships and virtues over the attractions of wealth and position.

Pip's general qualities are purposely somewhat vague. The changes in him are more important than his personality itself. He seems friendly, cheerful, generous, and above average intelligence. Dickens wished to send a normal, basically likable human being through the experiences involved in *Great Expectations*, and he, therefore, created Pip. Perhaps Pip remains likable, and retains the reader's sympathy so well even at the height of his snobbery and foolishness, because we can see so readily in him our own weaknesses and those of every person; as well as a person's redeeming qualities.

ESTELLA

Estella is an orphan like Pip, and she is brought up even more so than he outside of society and its usual patterns. She is shaped, from babyhood, by Miss Havisham. Estella becomes an instrument of Miss Havisham's and her true daughter in mind if not in body. Her name means star, and she is as aloof and cold as her namesake. When young, she learns her lessons well and takes to them, enjoying the feeling of superiority they give her. She must, like Pip, be imaginative as well. Estella has been as strongly influenced by her surroundings as by the old lady's teachings. Later on in the tale, when she and Pip are together in London, she often speaks of herself as being akin to a puppet—the control over her actions being in the hands of another. She speaks this calmly, so completely does she feel at one with Miss Havisham. At an indefinable point in the story, however, Miss Havisham lets go of the strings, and Estella continues on her own. We realize that it is she alone who is carrying on Miss Havisham's revenge—that she can live no other way and can relate to people in no other manner. She marries Drummle. He treats her with extreme cruelty before he is killed, making a widow of her. Throughout her life away from Miss Havisham, however, and despite her denials, the one person who is able to penetrate the fraud and ice that surround Estella is Pip. He is her confidant, and she warns him in a way that can only be interpreted as a sign of some kind of affection or regard. We can see her gradually softening in her increasing confidences to Pip, and, at their final meeting, we are somewhat prepared for what the great changes that have taken place in them both bring about. Estella, too, has suffered in her marriage to a brute and has experienced, to the full, a life of falsity and vindictive pretending. Perhaps Miss Havisham's death also contributed to the wisdom Estella gained through suffering. In the final lines, we feel that this cold and beautiful woman has been through much the same ordeal as Pip. She has learned also that the life she led was a miserable and empty one. As the novel closes, Estella, too, has become capable of love and true human feeling.

JOE

Joe Gargery is the one figure Dickens created in *Great Expectations* to take his stand opposed to, and apart from, the main current of the action. He stays away, for the most part, from London and all that happens in its world. He enters only when needed. He is always present, however, in the mind of Pip;

and Joe tends to peek out at odd moments to remind the reader (if not Pip himself) of those values and feelings Pip has trampled down in his new existence. Joe must seem to his neighbors much like what he seemed to Pip as a child: "a mild, good-natured, sweet-tempered, easy going, foolish, dear fellow." He is hard working and honest, and we learn that he believes in the virtues of industry. Joe is also naturally generous. This is illustrated clearly in his reply to the convict's statement that he stole some food from the blacksmith's house. Joe tells him that he was welcome to it if it kept a poor fellow creature from starving. Joe is also singular in the story in that he has no property. He regards all but the tools of his trade as belonging to Mrs. Joe. His freedom from material goods or desire for them sets him apart from the Pumblechooks and the "gentlemen" of the novel. We learn about Joe's childhood as he relates it to Pip. His father was a drunkard and beat both him and his mother often, causing them incredible hardship. Yet the epitaph that Joe had composed for his father reveals again his natural virtue in the sincere quality of his forgiveness. The epitaph, "Whatsume'er the failings on his part, Remember reader he were that good in his hart," could serve for Pip, as well, as he finishes his adventures.

Joe's significance in the novel goes far deeper than that of a virtuous and kindly blacksmith. His larger importance is indicated by Dickens' references to him, throughout, in religious terms. He is "holy" and he makes the cottage have an air of "sanctity" for Pip. Pip refers to him as "that gentle, Christian man." All these can serve as examples of Dickens' intentional conceptions of Joe throughout the story. Joe is opposed to all false values; not through windy speeches but within himself and his very presence, he seems to chase away the feelings of emptiness and gloom. Immediately he rejects the doctrines of the importance of property, pretty speech, and manners. He has, from the beginning, the wisdom that Pip suffers to obtain, and he is, at the same time, able to live in domestic love and tranquility. Joe also possesses a strong sense of honor and a dignity that Miss Havisham immediately senses. His understanding of people coupled with sensitivity enables him to sense immediately when he is not wanted by Pip or is making Pip uncomfortable by his presence. Socially, he stands at the base of the book and supports it, just as, in his character as a blacksmith, he stands at the base of society. The fire in his forge is the light of the innate goodness in humans; a light of hope amid the false lights of the world that Dickens presents to us in *Great Expectations.*

MISS HAVISHAM

We learn at one point in the novel that Miss Havisham was once beautiful and considered a great match. When we first meet her, however, that time has long passed, and she is a thin, frightening old woman whose entire life is now devoted to self-pity, to memories so bitter that they will not leave her, and to prideful revenge. She is mad, yes, but only in some respects. Even her madness is a sane and calculating one. Dickens has contrived to make her, and the house in which she lives, a unity; the aspect and conditions of the house are a clear reflection of Miss Havisham's mind. Decay is scattered about, time has stopped, and no light is allowed to enter through the barred windows. The darkness seems to nourish her and feed her passion for revenge. That Estella should carry out her vengeance is Miss Havisham's chief interest. Yet she also can be cruel in other, more petty, ways. She uses Pip to torment the relatives who plague her with false love and compliments. She deliberately encourages him in his mistaken idea that she is his benefactress and that Estella will be his. She does this despite her knowledge of the importance of these matters to him. She has been wronged and her pride, her shame, and her sensitive nature have let the wrong grow in the dark house until it has swelled out of all measure. She forgets everyone but herself and what she wishes; she is yet another example of pride and selfishness in the novel. She does not pause to consider Pip or his feelings. Actually, she did not pause to consider Estella's either; bringing much suffering to both of them.

Yet, early in the book, we begin to see some redeeming features in Miss Havisham's character. She does not treat Pip badly when he visits her, and she is able to recognize Joe as a trustworthy man of honor and principle. She also knows her relatives to be humbugs. Incidents like these prepare us for her final realization of the misery she has caused and her touching pleas for forgiveness. Her repentance is complete and Miss Havisham, as well as Pip and Estella, comes to a new knowledge of herself as *Great Expectations* draws to a close. For her, however, it is too late and there is no life left for her to live afresh. In Miss Havisham, Dickens has created one of those characters who looms so much larger than life. Her larger-than-life size is due to the immense energy of her passions and will.

MAGWITCH

Magwitch's first appearance on the scene is ferocious and sudden, but even during his threatening speech to Pip, he is somehow able to gain the reader's sympathy. It is worth noting that Magwitch does not say that he, himself, will eat the boy's heart and liver, but that another convict will do it. This convict does not exist as far as Magwitch knows. He does not wish to frighten the boy too much, yet he must frighten him enough to gain help in his desperate condition. Even here, his language is colorful. We see evidences of his good nature almost as soon as he is captured by the soldiers—in his statement that he stole the pie and other foodstuffs himself. We also see Magwitch, in the first stage of *Great Expectations*, as a man who has undergone and is undergoing much suffering and hardship. On his return to England, we begin to see him more clearly. He is as coarse and common as Joe but in a different way. He, like Joe, is a laboring man, but Magwitch has worked himself up to the point where he is a rich one. Although he has money, he still, somehow, is an object of pity, arriving with his long gray hair streaming about his creased face hoping to see his boy a gentleman. Magwitch's motives are clear. Above all is gratitude—a feeling that is notoriously

lacking in Pip. His idea of making Pip a gentleman, in gratitude, has expanded, however. Magwitch, too (like Pip and
Miss Havisham) is a victim of pride. He wishes to show the
world he makes as good a gentleman as anyone—as good a
gentleman as those colonists in Australia whose horses kicked
dust in his face as they rode by. Yet, he does not try to shape
Pip with such great selfishness as Miss Havisham exercises in
shaping Estella. He wants only simple pleasures out of his
creation—to be read to in foreign tongues and to be proud of
his boy's appearance and accomplishments.

Magwitch harbors resentment against the authorities and
Compeyson, but, in both cases, we feel that he is justified. He
is a brave man, fierce and single-minded when he returns to
England. These qualities, his obsession with Pip's being a
gentleman and his strange and wild appearance, make him
like Miss Havisham in as much as he becomes a figure far
larger than life. As the story draws to its close, we see Magwitch
on more human terms. He becomes more kindly and quieter.
He is always uncomplaining and trusting. He has grown old,
and, with Pip's becoming a gentleman and the final death of
Compeyson, his life is finished. He is able to accept, as God's
will, his death sentence in that ridiculous and horrible courtroom. On his deathbed, Magwitch is a broken man if we
compare him to what he once was. Yet, the breaking has
revealed a love and gentleness that his hard life had kept
concealed for years.

JAGGERS

Jaggers is another character in *Great Expectations* who
appears to Pip and the reader as larger than life. He is identified, from his first appearance, by his forefinger which
becomes a symbol of his authority and of the power he holds
over life and death. He is omnipotent in his sphere. He can
leave his house unlocked; he knows that no thief would dare
to rob him. He seems all-knowing as well for his appearance
declares him as one who has knowledge of the guilty secrets

of half of London. Wemmick states that Jaggers always looks as if he had set a man-trap and was watching it. A good measure of Jaggers' success is due, no doubt, to his knowledge of human nature and the guilt in all people. He is able to predict that Bentley Drummle will mistreat Estella. As a lawyer, his connection with crime makes him the perfect thematic vehicle for administering Pip's expectations. His achievements as a criminal lawyer also serve Dickens' purposes. They hold a revealing light to the law as practiced, to justice in England, and to the society that supports such systems. Jaggers is completely unscrupulous; he uses false witnesses and, no doubt, every other fraudulent tactic in the book. It is his business to defend the guilty, and he does it in a cold, efficient, and ruthless manner.

Jaggers has his other side as well. Yet, this other side is only hinted at. We can see him becoming somewhat attached to Pip. He has some ties with Wemmick and with Molly, his housekeeper, as well. His washing of his hands as his clients leave his office is indicative of his hypocrisy in his dealings with them. However, it also marks an effort on Jaggers' part to keep, somehow, personally clean of the filth in which he makes his living and to which he contributes. When Jaggers learns of Wemmick's home in Walworth and calls him a "cunning impostor," Wemmick says, "I think you're another." Wemmick continues by saying that he wouldn't be surprised if Jaggers might himself be planning a pleasant home one day. It is clear that Jaggers has compromised himself in order to earn a living and that there is another side to him. He nods and sighs before he speaks again to Pip. "Pip . . . we won't talk about 'poor dreams'; you know more about such things than I, having much fresher experience of that kind."

WEMMICK

John Wemmick's life, personality, and character are all neatly and firmly divided in two. That he finds this division necessary (in order to work in a lawyer's office and also maintain a pleasant home) is an unspoken comment by Dickens by which he condemns England's lawyers, judges, prisons, and laws themselves. When he is in Jaggers' office or the surrounding areas, Wemmick is described in inanimate terms. He is wooden, and his expression seems to have been chipped out with a chisel. His mouth reminds Pip of a mail slot, but we soon discover that Wemmick has another side to him; his office manner is for the office only. When Pip goes to Walworth, he sees Wemmick's pleasant and imaginatively constructed home and also his devotion to his aged father. Wemmick is a lover as well, and his marriage is gay and delightful. Many of the novel's finest comic scenes occur in Wemmick's Walworth castle home. He is also a man who works with his hands, and he tells Pip that he is his own "engineer . . . carpenter . . . plumber, and my own gardener . . ." Like Joe, he is emphatically not a gentleman. Wemmick is always practical, at Walworth as well as in the office, and he advocates the amassing of "portable property," although he does not think of it in the offensive manner of a Pumblechook. He becomes firm friends with Pip and advises him wisely on a few occasions. In relation to the rest of the characters in the novel, Wemmick's circumscribed life and mentality make him seem smaller than life size but no less alive. His diminutive stature as a character makes him an excellent balance against Jaggers. It is as though Wemmick were etched with a fine line; and Jaggers drawn with a broad, sweeping one.

CRITICAL COMMENTARY

EARLY CRITICISM

One of the first critical works to emerge dealing with the whole of Dickens' thought and achievement in fiction was Gilbert K. Chesterton's *Criticisms and Appreciations of Charles Dickens*, which appeared in 1911. Chesterton singles out *Great Expectations* as the one of Dickens' novels that stands alone for its "soft and gentle cynicism of old age." He makes the point that the book has no hero as do his earlier novels such as *David Copperfield* and *Oliver Twist*. Pip, despite all his virtues, is essentially unheroic, and we see as much, if not more, bad in him as we see good. Dickens sets out from the very beginning to present his character's weaknesses rather than his strengths. He is conscious that the great expectations to which he falls heir will be disappointing. Chesterton compares Dickens with George Eliot and William Thackeray, two other famous novelists of the same era. Using the incident in which Trabb's boy torments Pip, this critic attempts to define the quality in Dickens' writing that allows him to stand above these other authors as a greater artist. He tells us that the life, the "bounce," the indefinable vitality of a creation such as Trabb's boy (which Dickens gives us through a style that is able to move subtly along with the action being portrayed) is what sets Dickens above and apart from the other novelists of the Victorian Age. Chesterton also defends Dickens against the charges of sentimentality that had been made against him particularly where characters such as Joe Gargery are concerned. He feels that Joe was not "sweets" to Dickens but meat and bread, the true stuff of goodness in the people. Those critics who think him sweet and sentimental think so only because their own tastes run to the sour and the sophisticated. Chesterton feels that Dickens truly loved Joe's goodness and made him "a thing too obvious to be understood"; so straightforward and simple as to defy analysis.

The work of Chesterton was followed in 1947 by that of

Edmund Wilson, a critic who has exercised his talents in many fields. He tells us more of the relation of Dickens to his times and of how *Great Expectations* expresses its author's rebellious instincts. Wilson feels that Dickens distrusted the political and judicial systems of his England and was, invariably, in opposition to their institutions. We learn that he also distrusted the rising middle class of the early nineteenth century. Its puritanical virtues meant, for Dickens, the concealment of greed and exploitation, combined with a squelching of spontaneity, gaity, frankness, and all instinctive human virtues. In his novels, characters of this class do evil while pretending to do good; they work mischief as a matter of duty. Mr. Pumblechook, in *Great Expectations*, is obviously a prime example of this sort of man. Wilson points out that this book is like the earlier *David Copperfield* but in reverse. Instead of a gentleman accidentally turned into a laborer, a blacksmith's boy has a chance to become a gentleman. He also defines what he sees as the central problem or puzzle in the work. The money that will let Pip be a gentleman and rise out of poverty and ignorance ties him, at the same time, to even greater poverty and ignorance—to that of a criminal and a convict. Estella (the image of wealth and refinement he seeks) is discovered, correspondingly, to be the child of a convict and of a woman who was tried for murder. Wilson tells us that the central symbol in the book is stated in the title; it links the great expectations of both Pip and Estella to the Victorian optimism that surrounded Dickens in his life. This critic also reveals to us that *Great Expectations* represents an advance in the psychological treatment of characters in the work of Dickens. In his earlier novels, the proportions of good and evil were balanced within the book, but they rarely had equal sway in one character. Pip, however, passes through cycles in the book: he is at first sympathetic to us, then we grow to dislike him as he undergoes a process in which certain bad aspects of his character come to the fore, and, as the book ends, he is again sympathetic to the reader. We see the effects of riches from within and the effect of bringing together the high and the low. This dualism of high and low, rich and poor, good and bad, is marked by Wilson as a major theme in the works of Dickens as a whole as well as in *Great Expectations*.

MORE RECENT CRITICISM

An important book for the student of Dickens is Humphrey House's *The Dickens World*, which relates Dickens and his work to the social and political context in which he lived. House feels that Dickens, despite his many objections, was basically in sympathy with the ideas of progress current in his times. He would have agreed with Magwitch that money and education can produce a gentleman. Although House calls the book "a snob's progress," he feels that Dickens recognized that Pip emerges as a better man in the end for having had his great expectations. He is better spoken, he has a variety of interesting friends, and he does well in his business. The novel is, for House, "the perfect expression of a phase of English society," illustrating how money can change things and still has changed them for the better as the book ends. However, he also sees the book as a critique of this society and its pretensions. Pip's acquired culture really comes, upon close analysis, to little more than better speech, good table manners, and fancy clothes. It is not true cultural or educational advancement, and, although Pip reads much, we never find out what he is reading, and his reading clearly never has any real effect on his life or actions. Pip's progress indicates no genuine growth although it does effect a closing of the gap between classes—particularly between the upper and lower middle class. This greater class unity was rapidly occurring during Dickens' lifetime. It was due largely to the spread of public education. Although he himself is basically oriented toward sociological criticism, Humphrey House argues against the Marxist view of *Great Expectations* presented particularly by T. A. Jackson, who sees the novel as a treatise on the way in which the laboring classes are exploited by an aristocracy which is as little grateful to them as Pip is at first to Magwitch. House feels that relationships such as Pip's to Magwitch or to Trabb's boy have more meaning on a personal level.

George Orwell, in his book *Dickens, Dali, and Others*, makes a highly personal and none too complimentary statement along some of the same lines as Humphrey House. He also feels that Pip is better off as the book ends than he would have been at the forge. He criticizes Dickens for being hypocritical with himself. Orwell feels that, while professing to despise money and social position in the novel, Dickens actually had a lingering envy for both and an abhorrence for real poverty and social degradation. In this view, Dickens ultimately sees the greatest virtue in the class that Orwell sarcastically calls the "shabby genteel." In the class system of Victorian England, this would be Pip's final social status.

Edgar Johnson also views *Great Expectations* in social terms. He sees it, however, as a full-blown criticism of the values that Pip accepts as leading to a better way of life. Johnson claims that Dickens portrays these values harshly. He sensed that Pip's goals were actually to live a parasitic life on someone else's money, to avoid work, and to be in eternal and luxurious ease in a paradise of material goods. According to Johnson, Dickens' explorations of these values in *Great Expectations* shows up the life to which they lead as being false, empty, and cruel, involving loss of honor and humanity. He states: "The system of that society and its grandiose material dreams . . . involve a cheapening, a distortion, a denial of human values." The character of Jaggers also functions to reveal these same weaknesses in the social system. He can be a success in his profession only through hypocrisy, fraud, lies, and a total cutting off of his better, more human, self. The alternative present in the book is obvious; Johnson makes even more clear the position of Joe as the redeeming force in the novel. This judgment is reinforced, and it is pointed out that as the book ends, Pip too is a working man, as is Joe, although he is in a somewhat higher class.

Dorothy Van Ghent, in the section of her work, *The English Novel: Form and Function*, that deals with *Great Expectations* approaches the novel from a different point of view than those of the majority of the critics we have mentioned. She is interested chiefly in Dickens' technique and in his means of expression. Van Ghent begins her analysis by noting that Dickens' characters seem often to soliloquize when they should be carrying on a conversation with another person. She feels there is a lack of communication that shows itself most clearly when the dialogue is between people of two different social classes, two different age groups (a child and an old man, for example), or between people who have preconceived ideas or conclusions. Her examples of this lack of rapport (some of which can be easily argued with) include Pip's first conversation with Miss Havisham in which she asks him to "Play!," without understanding, in the least, the workings of the child's mind. She also mentions the conversation between Miss Havisham and Joe in which the latter addresses his remarks to Pip alone. Also, she mentions the point in the tale when Magwitch has Pip read to him in a language he cannot understand. To this list, the deaf Aged P. can easily be added. The only way for Pip to communicate with him is by nodding, and that venerable man is even guilty of a misunderstanding at his son's wedding. This absence of mutual comprehension is seen by Dorothy Van Ghent as an indication that Dickens saw and created for his readers a world in which people are essentially separate and isolated from one another. She sees, in *Great Expectations*, a world of frightening loneliness despite its humor. She tends to de-emphasize the instances of close communication in the book—the deep understanding of Biddy in her relationships with Pip and Joe, the communion of Pip and Herbert, and the final love between Pip and Magwitch. Dickens' abruptness of tempo in the novel adds fuel to Van Ghent's critical fire. She notes the number of sudden and strange confrontations that abound in this work of Dickens. Pip's meeting with the "pale young gentleman" (who offers to fight him for no reason), the sudden ferocious appearance of the convict on the marshes, and the arrival of the soldiers at Christmas dinner (just as Pip is in anguish over his theft) serve to illustrate her meaning. These collisions suggest to Van Ghent "the utmost incohesion in the stuff of experience," and are further indicators of a world of disorder. A chaos of random and frightening meetings between basically isolated and individual personalities forms the world in which this critic sees Pip. Despite a certain lack of careful reading in her analyses of thwarted communication, Van Ghent's sense of Dickens' method and of the total tone of the book is keen. One point that she makes strongly along these lines is Dickens' use of the pathetic fallacy (the attributing of personality and feeling to inanimate objects) and its opposite (portraying people in terms of inanimate objects) to express the inner life of his characters. She notes that Pip's sense of the convict and Miss Havisham is tied up with desolate marshes and that Wemmick can readily serve as an example of the dehumanization that depicting people in terms of objects implies. His mouth resembles a mail slot as long as he is in Little Britain with Jaggers.

One of the finest works on Dickens is Monroe Engel's book, *The Maturity of Dickens*. His section dealing with *Great Expectations* is entitled "The Sense of Self." It is in Pip and the changes in his mind and character that Engel finds the center of the novel. He sees Pip as a child in a state of original innocence, comparable to the innocence of Adam and Eve in the garden of Eden, in his life with Joe at the forge. He moves out of this innocence when he hears of his great expectations, and Engel feels that the novel is the account of his journey back to the garden, of his finding himself through experiences in which he suffers and learns much. In the final scene with Estella, he has returned to the ruins of Satis House, the ruins of what he thought was the source of his Eden. He is now ready to walk out with her and start his life anew. In the body of the book, Pip's love for Estella and his desire to be a gentleman run parallel in the linked themes of love and property. Both are extremely selfish desires for which he is willing to sacrifice Joe, Biddy, and his old nature. Until he becomes wise through his trials, he does not wish to give to others, but only to receive—whether it is Estella or money that is being presented to him. Sadly, Pip is used by both property and love rather than making use of them. In the end, however, Pip has learned to give as well as to work, like Joe, and to love truly rather than just to desire. Originally, Dickens had ended *Great Expectations* somewhat differently. Pip and Estella meet. It is obvious that Estella, like Pip, has had to learn to give. However, in the orginal ending, she has married a second time, and, as they part, Pip senses that they are irredeemably separate and that a phase of his life has come to a close. Engel feels that the ending Dickens finally chose is a bad one and regrets that Dickens changed it from its original form. He feels that, despite the cycle of images and changes in Pip that the second ending completes, it contradicts what is basically a novel of disillusion with false values and feelings. He also remarks, however, that the book proceeds through the serious and often frightening changes in Pip in a manner that is far from unhappy and reveals an undeniable zest for life.

Engel outlines the major themes of *Great Expectations* clearly for his readers: property (or money), love, and crime and justice. In the work, the differing attitudes toward property are expressed firmly in the personages of Joe, Mrs. Joe, Pumblechook, Wemmick, and Miss Havisham although property exerts its influence over the lives of everyone involved in the narrative. It is interesting to note, as Engel does, that it was Miss Havisham's property and wealth that first attracted Compeyson to her. He also points out that Dickens seems to feel that only a reasonable, rational love can succeed; those tinged with passion are doomed to failure. The love of Magwitch and Molly is in the latter category; as is the love of Pip for Estella in the central portion of the book. More reasonable love is represented by Joe and Biddy, Herbert Pocket and his Clara, and Wemmick and Miss Skiffins. An interesting and revealing point is also made by Engel concerning the theme of justice. He feels that Dickens created

Magwitch, in part at least, as a character who attempts the administration of good justice in contrast to that of the courts of law. Magwitch tries to reward good (Pip) and punish evil (Compeyson) in a direct and simple manner, and his attempts are both, in certain ways, successful. Engel's final judgment on *Great Expectations* emphasizes the social as well as the personal aspect of the novel. He states that the book "is subversive, and the power . . . depends on a response to the rendering of loss, of the beauty of hazard, of the horror of social injustice, and of the preposterous comedy of hypocrisy and self-delusion."

ESSAY QUESTIONS AND ANSWERS

Question

What do Mr. Pumblechook and Mr. Wopsle represent? What are their functions in the novel?

Answer

Pumblechook is a businessman, a corn and seed dealer. He is actually Joe's uncle, but he has been taken over by Mrs. Joe due to their common interests in property and in making the young Pip miserable. Throughout his childhood, Pumblechook is Pip's chief tormentor; flinging arithmetic problems at him, demanding that he be grateful to those who brought him up by hand, and predicting a bad end for him—on the gallows or worse. He is an insensate bully where Pip is concerned, making him feel guilty for being alive. In taking Pip to be bound as Joe's apprentice, he performs one of his greatest feats. He humiliates the boy completely and makes him feel like a criminal. When Pip comes into property, however, Pumblechook's fawning can be equalled only by his former browbeating. He brags insistently about his position as the founder of the boy's fortunes. When Pip is again without money, Pumblechook reverts to his former self, blaming Pip's fall on his "ingratitoode" to his first benefactor and to the founder of his fortunes. There is nothing good to be said about Pumblechook. He has no sensitivity to the feelings of others and no consciousness whatsoever of the existence of people as human beings. He can accuse Joe of "pigheadedness and ignorance"; he is completely selfish and a braggart who relates to people only for his own ends. He respects and responds only to the false values of money and position as these material acquisitions are to him the only things of worth that life offers. It is clear that Dickens means us to perceive that the existence of men like Pumblechook in the middle class makes possible the existence of such worthless gentlemen as Pip and Bentley Drummle.

Along with Pumblechook, Mr. Wopsle is one of Pip's child-hood tormentors. Wopsle is also selfish and proud to the point where he views the church, not as a place of worship, but as an arena in which he can shine in his speech and singing. Pip tries once to learn from him, but Wopsle, concerned with his own glory, succeeds in mauling the boy in a poetic fury rather than in teaching him anything. When he enters the theater, Wopsle is also ridiculous for he attempts acting in the manner in which he attempts everything else. He is vain, self-centered, and conscious only of his own pomp and circumstance. He is utterly unable to see the all-too-obvious fact of his performance's failure. He cannot think of his acting as bad and places the blame on the audience. He is patronizing and condescending to his dresser at the theater. Mr. Wopsle is less offensive to us than Mr. Pumblechook if only because he sometimes seems pitiful. He is a prime example of lack of self-awareness, pomposity, and false pretences. He and Mr. Pumblechook stand as two men who epitomize the worst vices of the social situation in England as Dickens saw it. Pumblechook's hypocrisy and superior attitudes and Wopsle's pretensions and foolishness reflect both on society in general and on Pip himself, who acquires their vices along with his great expectations.

Question

In what light are law, justice, and their representatives presented in *Great Expectations?* How do they relate to the central meaning of the story?

Answer

Justice is most often presented in this novel in terms of punishment. Our first view of it is our view of the Hulks and of the old gallows on the marshes. These arise as strong symbols, the Hulks in particular, of the horrors of prison and the severity of justice in condemning men to such a place. We soon meet agents of the law themselves in the persons of the soldiers who are hunting the escaped convicts. Joe and Pip hope that the convicts escape, and we sense a leaning on the part of Dickens toward the side of the criminal in his battle against the law. This is the first note sounded in the novel's use of crime and criminals as symbols of revolt against a given order in society or in personal relations. We are first taken to the courts of justice themselves when Pip is bound as an apprentice, and the impression given us of the judicial system is none too favorable: "and with mighty Justices (one with a powdered head) leaning back in chairs, with folded arms, or taking snuff, or going to sleep, or writing, or reading the newspapers." Jaggers, with his power to cheat justice at will, makes even greater mockery of law. He plays on the universal sense of guilt, on the criminal in all people, and the judges and magistrates cannot but shiver and quake before him, seeming sillier and more ineffectual than ever. In Magwitch's narrative, justice is at fault again for it gives the greater villain, Compeyson, a much lighter sentence because he seems like a gentleman. At the trial of Magwitch himself, Dickens creates a religious atmosphere in the courtroom that contrasts violently with what occurs there: thirty-two deaths are decreed. The feeling of mercy, felt so strongly by Pip and Joe in the marshes, has no place in this framework of justice.

The social implications of this criticism of the law courts and the penal system are clear and the same condemnations appear in other novels of Dickens, *Bleak House* and *Little Dorrit* in particular. Dickens states in *Great Expectations* that "jails were much neglected." A society too occupied with "progress" and material goods to improve its prisons and courts is not a sound one. This implication echoes throughout the novel. The foolishness of justice and the positive symbolic position of the criminal emphasize the sense of almost total confusion and the lack of knowledge concerning right and wrong in this world. It is the criminals who do justice in *Great Expectations*—Orlick in his buffeting of Pumblechook and Magwitch in his love for Pip and vengeance on Compeyson. If a criminal stands apart from society's rules and procedures, then Joe is a criminal as well. This is clearly not the case, and, just as clearly, the rules and procedures that make men's laws and govern their minds are wrong. It is these rules and mores that lead Pip into a life of crime; for the real criminal, the real target for justice according to Dickens, is the man who forsakes all true human feelings and ties, in order to have a hand in wealth and a sense of superiority. Dickens feels clearly that law and justice must first carefully judge themselves before they judge others.

Question

How do contrasting images of light and dark reinforce meaning in the novel?

Answer

Images of light and dark in *Great Expectations* are used by Dickens to increase the clarity of line between good and evil. These images also serve as a stylistic device; infusing the plot with greater unity and serving as consistent symbols of certain characters or places. For example, when certain characters and places are all identified by light rather than dark, we perceive them as related forces tending to operate in similar directions.

The initial images of darkness in the book are the marshes, the Hulks, and the mist. These images recur frequently in the body of the novel and deepen the sense of dread through their linking of the presently occurring scene with earlier ones. The mist gives way to light at Pip's departure to London. It does the same again in the story's final lines. In Pip's meeting with Orlick at the lime-kiln, the mist is heavy as it was when he first met Magwitch. One of the novel's chief places of darkness is Satis House where the sun is never allowed to penetrate and where the fire smolders only in the grate. Estella is part of this darkness as well although she holds a candle in it. This is an indication of her final rebirth and of a life within her that cannot be completely given to Miss Havisham. The evil Orlick is a creature of the dark and the mist. He seems to appear suddenly out of them and disappears as if he could become one with them. Bentley Drummle, too, is a creature of the dark. Pip reveals this in his talk about their boating. "Bentley Drummle came up in our wake alone, under the overhanging banks and among the rushes . . . and I always think of him as coming after us in the dark or by the back water, when our own row boats were breaking the sunset or the moonlight in midstream." When Magwitch comes to see Pip, bringing with him the destruction of all Pip's expectations, the staircase lights are out, and Pip has only a reading lamp by which to see him.

The imagery of light (and of light breaking up the darkness) first appears vividly with the soldiers who carry torches to guide them in their search on the dark marshes. Minor images of light, used to describe positive people or places, abound in the novel. These include Startop, with his bright face; Estella in Satis House with her candle, and Wemmick with his cannon at Walworth. However, two images of the light that burns in darkness stay with a reader long after *Great Expectations* has been concluded. Miss Havisham, in the darkness of her decaying house, at the very moment after she realizes the enormity of her sins and her great need for forgiveness, becomes a "great flaming light" as her dress catches fire from the embers. Miss Havisham's realization, although it has come too late, redeems her. The fire is a symbol of that redemption. The other memorable fire is, of course, that of Joe's forge. Joe is blond as well and is a central image of light throughout the work. Dickens has created him in such a way that, when light is streaming out from his forge across the road in the darkness, we feel it is not only the forge fire, but Joe's radiance as well, that illumines the night. In much the same way as his fire lights the road, his very presence in Pip's sickroom lightens it and gives new life to the invalid. Joe's humanity offers the only redemption in a darkly sinful world.

Question

Miss Havisham makes Estella into a lady, and Magwitch makes Pip a gentleman. Compare their methods, motives, and results.

Answer

There are many parallels between the careers of Pip and Estella—orphans transformed into figures fit for society. In these two careers lies much of the meaning of *Great Expectations*. The methods of Magwitch and Miss Havisham are remarkably similar excepting, of course, the special teachings that Miss Havisham imparts to her adopted daughter. It is money, and a certain basic education in speech and manners that turn the trick, and the reader feels (along with Dickens) that a trick so turned must end in disaster. The motives of Magwitch and Miss Havisham, the two molders of people, are also similar. They both act through injured pride: Miss Havisham was jilted by Compeyson, and Magwitch was treated badly by colonial gentlemen and Compeyson, the phony gentleman. Also, they both wish revenge for these injuries. For Miss Havisham, the triumph in her revenge is far more direct. Magwitch must be content to revenge himself through the satisfaction of having made a better gentleman than them all. However, Magwitch also acts through genuine gratitude and, later, out of true affection for Pip. Miss Havisham has no such motive where Estella is concerned, but she does develop a strange and deep rapport with the girl; feeling Estella's destiny as her own.

The results of the creations in both cases are very clear. Estella's becoming what she is results in the heartsick grief of a repentant Miss Havisham and an ordeal of suffering for Estella herself. Pip becomes an ingrate and a snob as he becomes a gentleman, and only by death is Magwitch preserved from the knowledge of his gentleman's multi-fold failure. In creating two people able to move easily in society, and in showing their inevitable failures at living true lives, Dickens makes the point that the goal of the such shaping is a false one. It asks human beings to forget the stuff of life for an existence that is empty, showy, foolish, and, in Estella's case, dangerous to those around her. If Magwitch and Miss Havisham had chosen weaker people, people (in the last analysis) less sincere and less capable of being true to themselves, they might have succeeded. They chose human beings who possessed fair portions of the natural human virtues and emotions, and their experiments were doomed to failure.

BIBLIOGRAPHY

Chesterton, Gilbert K. *Criticisms and Appreciations of Charles Dickens*. New York: E. P. Dutton & Co., 1911.

Chesterton, Gilbert K. *Charles Dickens*. New York: Schocken Books, 1965.

Collins, Philip A. W. *Dickens and Crime*. New York: St. Martin's Press, 1962.

Cruikshank, Robert James. *Charles Dickens and Early Victorian England*. New York: Chanticleer Press, 1949.

Davis, Earle Roscoe. *The Flint and the Flame; the Artistry of Charles Dickens*. Columbia: University of Missouri Press, 1963.

Du Cann, Charles G. L. *The Love-Lives of Charles Dickens*. London: F. Muller, 1961.

Engel, Monroe. *The Maturity of Dickens*. Cambridge, MA: Harvard University Press, 1959.

Fielding, K. J. *Charles Dickens: A Critical Introduction*. New York: David McKay Co., 1958.

Ford, George Harry. *Dickens and His Readers*. Princeton, NJ: Princeton University Press, 1955.

Forster, John. *The Life of Charles Dickens*, 2 vols. New York: E.P. Dutton, 1928.

Hagan, John H., Jr. "The Poor Labyrinth: The Theme of Social Injustice in Dickens's *Great Expectations*." *Nineteenth Century Fiction*, IX, 3 (December 1954).

Hill, T. W. "Notes on '*Great Expectations*.'" *Dickensian*, LIV (1958).

House, Humphrey. *The Dickens World*, 2nd ed. New York: Oxford University Press, 1960.

Jackson, T. A. *Charles Dickens: The Progress of a Radical*. New York: International Publishers, 1948.

Johnson, Edgar. *Charles Dickens: His Tragedy and Triumph*, 2 vols. New York: Simon and Schuster, 1953.

Johnson, Edgar. "Dickens and Shaw: Critics of Society." *Virginia Quarterly* Review, XXXIII (1957).

Leacock, Stephen. *Charles Dickens: His Life and Work*. Garden City, NY: Doubleday, Doran and Co., 1934.

Ley, J. W. T. *The Dickens Circle*. London: Chapman and Hall, Ltd., 1919.

Lindberg, John. "Individual Conscience and Social Injustice in *Great Expectations*." *College English*, XXIII (1961).

Miller, J. Hillis. *Charles Dickens: The World of His Novels*. Cambridge, MA: Harvard University Press, 1958.

Moynahan, Julian. "The Hero's Guilt: The Case of *Great Expectations*." *Essays in Criticism*, X, 1 (January 1960).

Nisbet, Ada. *Dickens and Ellen Ternan*. Berkeley: University of California Press, 1952.

Orwell, George. *Dickens, Dali, and Others*. New York: Harcourt, Brace, 1946.

Parish, Charles. "A Boy Brought Up 'By Hand.'" *Nineteenth Century Fiction*, XVII (1961).

Partlow, Robert B., Jr. "The Moving I: A Study of the Point of View in *Great Expectations*." *College English*, XXIII, 2 (November 1961).

Pearson, Hesketh. *Dickens: His Character, Comedy, and Career*. New York: Harpers, 1949.

Pope-Hennessy, Una. *Charles Dickens 1812–1870*. London: Howell, Soskin, 1946.

Spilka, Mark. *Dickens and Kafka: A Mutual Interpretation*. Bloomington: Indiana University Press, 1963.

Van Ghent, Dorothy. *The English Novel: Form and Function*. New York: Holt, Rinehart and Winston, 1953.

Wilson, Edmund. *The Wound and the Bow*. New York: Oxford University Press, 1947.

NOTES

NOTES

NOTES

NOTES

NOTES

NOTES

NOTES

NOTES

NOTES

NOTES